gi-tli gos GUO
do HUNDUR IHA-CHA-EH keu
kalbu KALBuM KAO kelb kuc
R Koira KOLII kringmerk kyne MA
ER KUTTA KUTYA n
R kuon kutro KUTTA KUTYA n
AH maile mbwa mengikuti pe
NTJA OBLKD okeraman PAPAS Pek pe
IES QAN Qen CALB QIMUGTA R1KONO SO
SEG seta shkukur SKYLOS Wul
ay SUNIS suns tti txakur
NDU aja aku ALLCU Animosh ANJING
lb can cane Canichien dzahhlieey e
au gi-tli gos GUOK Hansi hansi kku
hundo HUNDUR IHA-CHA-EH Imbwa i
kalbu KALBuM KAO kelb kuche
KOLII kringmerk kyne MADD
KUTYA kyne
ti nki

THIS
BOOK
WILL
CHANGE
YOUR
DOG'S
LIFE

STIMULATING CANINE CHALLENGES
TO ENSURE EVERY DOG HAS ITS DAY

Copyright © The Ivy Press Limited 2009

First Lyons Press edition, 2009

The Lyons Press is an imprint of
The Globe Pequot Press.

Creative Director Peter Bridgewater
Publisher Jason Hook
Editorial Director Tom Kitch
Senior Editor Lorraine Turner
Art Director Wayne Blades
Design and Illustrations Clare Barber, Joanna Clinch,
Renaldo Davison, Clare Harris, Kate Haynes, Tonwen
Jones, Joanna Kerr, JC Lanaway, Caroline Marklew,
Jon Raimes, Sarah Skeate
Text Viv Croot and Andrew Kirk

10 9 8 7 6 5 4 3 2 1

Printed in China
ISBN 978-1-59921-499-3

Library of Congress Cataloging-in-Publication
Data is available on file.

DISCLAIMER

Readers are warned not to follow any of the
advice or instructions given in this book. If
they do, we must point out that it is entirely at
their own risk and nothing to do with us.

Guarantee

THIS IS YOUR GUARANTEE
THAT THIS BOOK WILL
CHANGE
YOUR DOG'S LIFE*

Passed with flying colors

Summa cum Laude

DAY 1: SIGN IN

Name ....

Kennel Name ....

Breed ....

Address ....

....

....

....

Star Sign ....

Favorite Tree ....

Your photograph here

PAW PRINTS

FRONT LEFT PAW HERE

Things I Love

- ☐
- ☐
- ☐
- ☐
- ☐
- ☐
- ☐

Things I Hate

- ☐
- ☐
- ☐
- ☐
- ☐
- ☐
- ☐

BACK LEFT PAW HERE

Mission Statement:

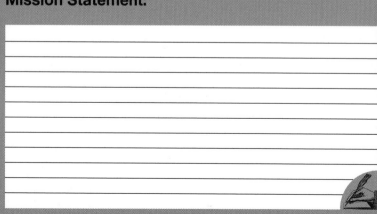

My Prizes

Boost your dog's self-esteem by displaying any awards he has won here. If there are more than three, go to the end of the book, where there is more display space.

MY HUMAN

Name ....

Gender ....

Disposition ....

....

....

....

....

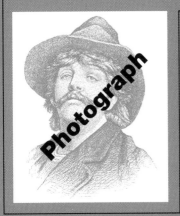

Photograph

How to Use This Book

This book contains 365 transformative activities to cover every day of the year, starting today. You and your dog must do the tasks in the order presented. Finish each task before moving on. Obviously you will need to help your dog with many of the projects, but the idea is that by the time you have got to the end of the book he or she will be a more autonomous, envelope-pushing sort of canine ready to take on new challenges. The first task is to fill in these pages. You do the writing part of it, and stick in the photographs of you and your dog—your dog does the paw prints. Take great care over the Mission Statement. What do you and your dog really want to achieve?

LOOKALIKE

It is said that all **owners come to look like their dogs and vice versa**.

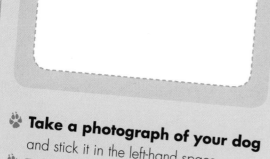

- 🐾 **Take a photograph of your dog** and stick it in the left-hand space.
- 🐾 **Take a photograph of yourself** and stick it in the right-hand space.
- 🐾 **Now note similarities and differences**, using highlighters and leader lines to show your workings.
- 🐾 **You can repeat the exercises in a year's time**, on a separate sheet of paper, to **see how you and your dog have progressed**.

Hints and Tips

- Try out both full-face shots and profiles to see if the likeness is expressed as an angle.
- Keep backgrounds uncluttered, and use the same one for both of you.
- Shave your beard off.
- Don't wear garish clothes (or leads).
- Don't try to look cute or appealing on purpose.
- Keep your eyes open.

Wannabes

Many dogs look like famous human celebrities: Winston Churchill, Richard Nixon, W.H. Auden, Celine Dion. Spend happy hours looking through magazines and websites to find out who your dog looks like.

You Ain't Nothin' But a Hound Dog

DAY 3

DAY 2

Dress yourself and your dog as Elvis (black leather or Vegas); go to the park with your music player. Place a collecting hat in front of the dog and mime to Elvis's greatest hits. Aim to collect $18.35* exactly. Stop when you have achieved it. Use the money to open a bank account for your dog.

*This is Elvis's birth date (1/8/35) in money.

DAY 4

Nipper Channeling

Nipper was the dog on the His Master's Voice label. Improve your dog's mind by playing him classical music for an hour. Make him sit still and listen, with one of those funnel collars on.

DAY 5

movie dogs

Get together with other owners and their dogs and show a dog-themed movie. Take it in turn to cater to all tastes. Here are some suggestions: *Ghost Dog, Dog Day Afternoon, The Day of the Jackal, Wag the Dog, Best in Show, My Life as a Dog, Dog Soldiers, Amor es Perros, Un Chien Andalou.*

Are you going to bark all day doggy or are you going to bite?

Is your dog really a Dog?

According to the Chinese zodiacal system, everyone is assigned to an animal, depending on their year of birth. There are only twelve of these animals and only one of them is a Dog.

IF YOUR DOG WAS BORN
January 25, 1982–February 12, 1983
(probably a deceased dog)
February 10, 1994–January 30, 1995
January 29, 2006–February 17, 2007

He is actually a Dog. Your next chance for a Dog dog is between February 6, 2018 and February 4, 2019.

DOG
Jan 25, 1982–
Feb 12, 1983
Feb 10, 1994–
Jan 30, 1995
Jan 29, 2006–
Feb 17, 2007

ROOSTER
Jan 23, 1993–
Feb 9, 1994
Feb 9, 2005–
Jan 28, 2006

MONKEY
Feb 4, 1992–
Jan 22, 1993
Jan 22, 2004–
Feb 8, 2005

SHEEP
Feb 15, 1991–
Feb 3, 1992
Feb 1, 2003–
Jan 21, 2004

HORSE
Jan 27, 1990–
Feb 14, 1991
Feb 12, 2002–
Jan 31, 2003

SNAKE
Feb 6, 1989–
Jan 26, 1990
Jan 24, 2001–
Feb 11, 2002

狗 鸡 猴 羊 马 蛇

Dogs born in any other years are Pigs, Rats, Oxen, Tigers, Rabbits (or Cats), Dragons, Snakes, Horses, Sheep (or Goats), Monkeys, or Roosters (or Chickens). Look up your dog's birth in our handy chart, and then make him an appropriate mask or disguise to empower his hidden Chinese animal.

PIG

Feb, 13 1983–
Feb 1, 1984

Jan 31, 1995–
Feb 18, 1996

Feb 18, 2007–
Feb 6, 2008

RAT

Feb 2, 1984–
Feb 19, 1985

Feb 19, 1996–
Feb 7, 1997

Feb 7, 2008–
Jan 25, 2009

OX

Feb 20, 1985–
Feb 8, 1986

Feb 8, 1997–
Jan 27, 1998

Jan 26, 2009–
Feb 13, 2010

TIGER

Feb 9, 1986–
Jan 28, 1987

Jan 28, 1998–
Feb 15, 1999

RABBIT

Jan 29, 1987–
Feb 16, 1988

Feb 16, 1999–
Feb 4, 2000

DRAGON

Feb 17, 1988–
Feb 5, 1989

Feb 5, 2000–
Jan 23, 2001

DAY 8

OUTSOURCE YOUR DOG'S JOBS: 1

FETCHING

Fetcher required for overcommitted family dog who is temperamentally and physically unsuited to fetching for himself.

SKILLS REQUIRED

- I am a robust owner who can throw sticks long distance so strong legs essential.
- Low boredom threshold.
- Willingness to fetch objects of all shapes, sizes and texture.
- Own teeth.
- Accuracy of positioning when dropping object at owner's foot.

FROST CALCULATOR

Wanted: Dog with inbuilt resistance to low temperature environments to measure frost levels in malfunctioning freezers. Own protective fur and frost-resistant foot pads essential. Would particularly suit Siberian huskies, Alaskan malamutes, and samoyeds.

GRASS SEED GRADER

Wanted: Allergy-free dog with a light touch and perfect eyesight required to grade grass seeds for use in national parks across the United States.

DAY 9

DAY 10

AWAY DAY

?

Go to the local bus or train station. Get on the first bus or train you see that's going somewhere he's never been before. See if he can find his own way back.

Day 11

DOG STAR

Photograph your dog in six incidents from your favorite episode of *Lassie/Old Yeller/Rin-Tin-Tin/The Littlest Hobo*. Stick them in the spaces provided.

Today, let your dog teach you:
HOW TO CATCH A FRISBEE USING YOUR TEETH.

FRISBEE CATCHING

RULES OF CONTACT

→ Walk to the park carrying a Frisbee in your mouth.

→ When you get there, drop it to the ground and stare at it. Eventually someone will throw it for you.

→ As soon as it leaves the thrower's hand, run very fast in the direction of the throw.

→ Calculating windspeed as you go, jump up as the Frisbee comes down—keep your mouth open.

→ Snap on the Frisbee and clamp jaws shut. Run back with it to the thrower and drop it at his/her feet.

→ NB: If you miss the Frisbee and clamp jaws shut, just chase after it, get down on all fours, and pick it up with your teeth.

Make me proud

Live Fast

Day 13

Live life to the fullest. Treat every minute as an hour. Follow this timetable, starting at 8:00 am in the morning.

8:00 Get up
8 and 30 seconds Eat breakfast, and feed your dog
8:01 Play with squeaky toy
8:01 and 30 seconds First walk
8:02 Do some work and leave dog in basket
8:04 Cup of coffee, dog treat
8:06 Eat lunch
8:07 Play frisbee in park
8:09 Cup of tea, dog treat
8:11 Eat dinner
8:12 Watch TV
8:13 Late walk
8:14 Bath if necessary
8:15 Nightcap and last trip around the block
8:16 Bed and basket

Get up at 8:24 and start Day 2.

DAY 14

Placebo Your Dingo

Tell your dog you are giving him Viagra to increase his lust for life. Give him a multivitamin tablet instead, taking care that he does not see the package. See how many more legs, tree stumps, or cars he humps. Report your findings to the Proceedings of the Veterinarians Society.

Goth Dog

Let your dog access his inner goth. Purchase black dog bowls and install stained glass windows in his kennel.

DAY 16

IMPOSSIBLE TRICKS 1

TODAY YOU AND YOUR DOG WILL ATTEMPT TO MASTER ONE **IMPOSSIBLE** TRICK.

GET CELL RECEPTION IN A DEAD ZONE.

DOG PHRENOLOGY

Feel your dog's bumps. Let him feel yours.

DAY 18

Be worth it

Some dogs produce a great deal of drool. Don't let it go to waste or just stain the rug. Collect it and recycle it as hair gel. Start as a niche product, become famous via word of mouth and exclusivity, and sell out to L'Oréal. You and the dog can retire to Malibu.

DAY 19 | **Ecodog 1**

Your dog pants all day, right? So fit him up with some motion sensors on his chest, which are wired to a kinetic energy cell. Instant free electricity! You can use him as a handy generator for camping trips.

DAY 20

Masterclass 2

HOW TO SCRATCH BEHIND YOUR EAR

Let your dog teach you
ANOTHER OF HIS TRICKS.

DAY 21

Doggy SNAPS

Make a holiday photo **story** by **photographing** your **dog** with **props** to **capture** the different **times** of the day and different **activities** you did on **vacation.**

place your dog image here

place your dog image here

place your dog image here

place your dog image here

place your dog image here

place your dog image here

Know Your Vet

Visiting the vet is very scary for your dog. So help him out by familiarizing him with the vet and his examination room before he goes there. You can use flash cards. Make sure they show...

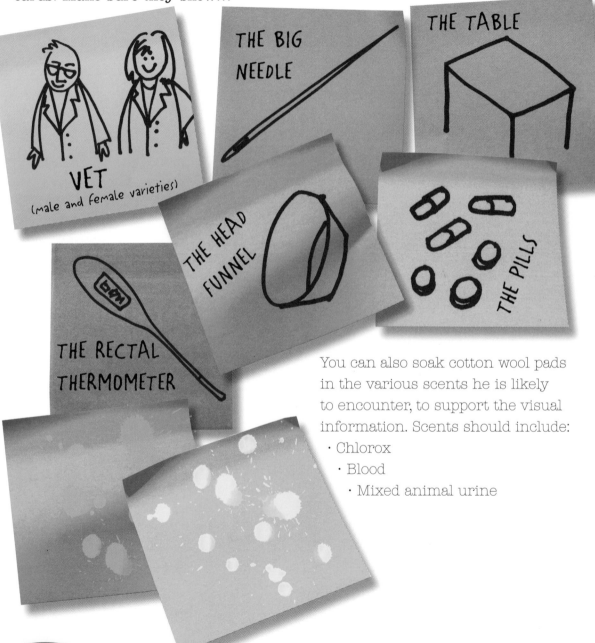

VET
(male and female varieties)

THE BIG NEEDLE

THE TABLE

THE HEAD FUNNEL

THE PILLS

THE RECTAL THERMOMETER

You can also soak cotton wool pads in the various scents he is likely to encounter, to support the visual information. Scents should include:
· Chlorox
· Blood
· Mixed animal urine

DAY 22

FAIRGROUND

The Doge Leonardo Loredan, 1501–4, Giovanni Bellini (d. 1516)

FUN

Doge of Venice Screen

Make a fairground-inspired screen, using a famous dog-style painting and some garish paint. Let your dog stick his head through.

SING IT!

You know how in those cheesy musicals, people are always bursting into song on very flimsy rationale either because their best girl/boy does/doesn't love them, or because they are gonna grease their car all over with a bunch of like-minded friends to make it go faster, or just to inform everybody that the road they intend to follow is made of yellow bricks, like we care? Well, why should your dog miss out? We're not saying write a musical, but you could, you know, burst into appropriate song and do the show right here every time you and your dog meet, write it all down, go Off-Broadway. You never know, It worked for Cats.

DAY 25

DOG CAM

Strap a camera on your dog's head and go out into the streets. You can either:

1 Stream it straight onto the net.
2 Examine it before it goes out and think about blackmailing options.
3 Show it at the Sundance film festival.

DOG BATIK

Make your own interesting ethnic fabric with your dog.

Day 26

1. Obtain undyed fabric.

2. Paint patterns on it in hot wax.

3. Dip your dog in vegetable dye.

4. Encourage him to roll about in the fabric in a random manner.

5. When he is bored, remove the fabric and iron it under paper to melt out all the wax.

6. Sell at your local green market.

DAY 27

Bone In

BARK FM

CALL HOWARD STERN/RUSH LIMBAUGH/DON IMUS, OR YOUR LOCAL EQUIVALENT, AND LET YOUR DOG DISCUSS CONTENTIOUS ISSUES WITH HIM. IF YOUR DOG IS ANY GOOD HE WILL SOON HAVE HIS OWN SHOW.

YOUR COUNTRY NEEDS YOU (AND YOUR DOG)

Sign yourself and your dog up for a tour of duty.

If you don't like fighting, just volunteer the dog.

CITIZEN DOG 1

BARKING MAD PARTY

REGISTER YOUR DOG TO VOTE:

- 🐾 Dress him in appropriate togs on polling day.

- 🐾 See if he can CHANGE THE COURSE OF HISTORY.

Day 30 Revolution

Let out your dog's inner rebel.
Let him spend the day as
Ernesto Che Guevara

Other revolutionaries are available:
Bernardo O'Higgins, liberator of Chile;
Simon Bolivar, liberator of the northern
part of South America; Dolores Ibarruri
Gomez (La Pasionaria), heroine of the
Spanish Civil War.

NB If your dog is a Basque Shepherd
Dog (Euskal artizan Txakurra), he
may be particularly excited about this
because all these revolutionaries have
Basque connections.

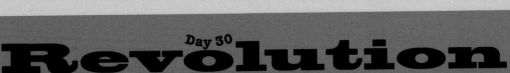

DAY 31

CITIZEN DOG 2

Take your dog to scent mark as many significant national monuments as possible. This will encourage his sense of national identity and obviate the danger of his being radicalized by a terrorist cell

LINCOLN MEMORIAL
National Mall, Washington, D.C., Henry Bacon, 1922

THE PENTAGON
Arlington, Virginia, George Bergstrom, 1943

US MARINE CORPS WAR MEMORIAL
Arlington National Cemetery, Virginia, Felix de Weldon, 1954

STATUE OF LIBERTY
Liberty Island, New York Harbor, Frédéric Auguste Bartholdi, 1886

THE WHITE HOUSE
Pennsylvania Avenue, Washington, D.C., James Hoban, 1800

MOUNT RUSHMORE
Keystone, South Dakota, Gutzon Borglum, 1941

DAY 32

KNOW YOUR FLEAS

Teach your dog about his fleas. It may help him scratch less.

a dogumentary

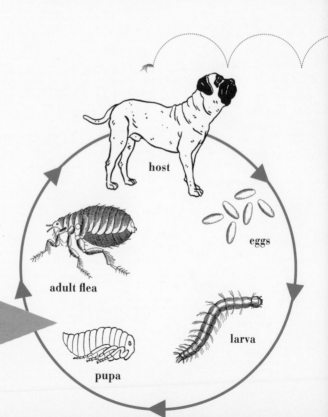

host

eggs

larva

pupa

adult flea

Pooperscooper Challenge

Today you will scoop your dog's poop using the following items ONLY: Two coffee spoons; a borrowed glove; a $10 note.

POOP TYPE	SCOOP TOOL	TIME TAKEN

DAY
33

Maître du chow

You enjoy wine tasting. Why not train your dog's palate by hosting a blind chow tasting session for your dog? Maybe invite a few select friends of his who can be relied on not to eat the bowl as well. Set out six bowls containing various brands of dog food, from hand cooked to a cheapo supermarket brand. (Don't forget to label them.) Go for meat or kibble, do not mix. Blindfold your dog, then make careful notes about the dishes he favors. This will encourage more discriminatory eating habits and maybe save you a buck or two if a cheaper brand wins out, and goes to show that it's you who is seduced by slick marketing, not your dog.

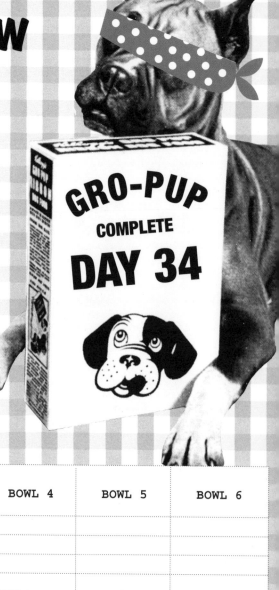

BOWL 1	BOWL 2	BOWL 3	BOWL 4	BOWL 5	BOWL 6

DAY 35

ROAD SENSE 1

TEST YOUR LEVEL OF TRAFFIC AWARENESS. Take your usual walk together but let the dog wear a blindfold. If the dog gets run over, you fail the test.

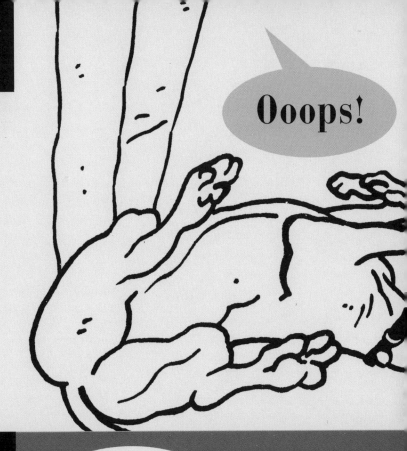

DAY 36

ROAD SENSE 2

TEST YOUR DOG'S LEVEL OF TRAFFIC AWARENESS. Take your usual walk together but you wear a blindfold. If you get run over, the dog fails the test.

EXPLOIT YOUR DOG NO. 2

As a book end

Choose a smaller, heavier breed with sedentary habits for this task, especially one that lacks the imagination to disobey when you give the command "stay."

Make your dog feel inferior: 1

Find a picture of noble rescue dogs heroically saving lives. Choose a snapshot of your dog looking his most fat and lazy and superimpose it into the image. Hang it in his kennel/basket to motivate him to do something about his slobby lifestyle and get in training to be a hero.

OUT DAMNED SPOT

Perform an exorcism on your dog. You can't be too careful. You will need a bell, a book, a candle, and a Max von Sydow impersonator.

FLASH DOGS

Secretly scatter anise at random places in your neighborhood. Then film the resultant canine flash mobs that appear and post on the Internet.

DAY 40

Paper moon

Dogs like to howl at the moon. On nights when there is no moon, or to entertain dogs who live in areas of maximum light pollution (where the moon is invisible), create an artificial moon for him to bay at.

YOU WILL NEED:

- 🐾 Large balloon
- 🐾 Old newspapers
- 🐾 Flour and water glue
- 🐾 Luminous silvery white spray paint

STEP ONE: Blow up balloon and tie a long string on it.

STEP TWO: Create a papier mâché moon by layering newspapers over the balloon, gluing together with flour and water glue.

STEP THREE: When your moon is dry, spray it silver.

STEP FOUR: Make smudges to represent the Sea of Tranquillity, etc.

STEP FIVE: Tie the moon up in prominent position so your dog can see it.

STEP SIX: Shine your flashlight onto the moon to represent the Sun's rays.

STEP SEVEN: Enjoy the howling.

Dog Sinister

Spend the day with your dog, turning left whenever a choice presents itself. Make a long straight run first of all, because otherwise you will be back home very speedily.

KEEP LEFT

Confessional

GET DRUNK with your dog and see if he tells you something **HE HAS NEVER TOLD ANYONE ELSE BEFORE.**

Mood Chart

Your dog does not behave the same way every day. Some days he is ecstatic to see the old rubber bone in his basket. Other days, he kicks it out. Take the uncertainty out of your lives by creating a mood chart. At the end of each day, fill it in with your dog. Keep the mood chart going for four weeks; you should see a pattern emerging and can work out the optimum time to teach tricks, go out, etc.

DAY 44

MOOD	00.00	01.00	02.00	03.00	04.00	05.00	06.00	07.00	08.00	09.00	10.00	11.00	12.00	13.00	14.00	15.00	16.00	17.00	18.00	19.00	20.00	21.00	22.00	23.00
ASLEEP																								
BARKING																								
PLAYING																								
KEEN																								
DULL																								
ANGRY																								
SOPPY																								
ENERGETIC																								
LETHARGIC																								
SEXUALLY AROUSED																								
SULKY																								

TIME

Life Coach
Your Dog

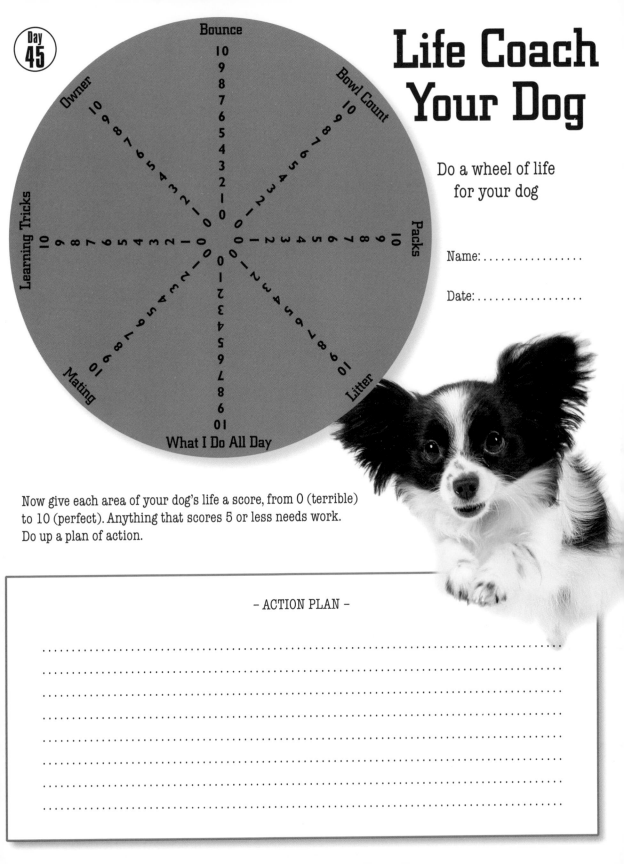

Bounce

Bowl Count

Owner

Learning Tricks

Packs

Mating

Litter

What I Do All Day

Do a wheel of life
for your dog

Name: . . . .

Date: . . . .

Now give each area of your dog's life a score, from 0 (terrible)
to 10 (perfect). Anything that scores 5 or less needs work.
Do up a plan of action.

– ACTION PLAN –

. . . .

. . . .

. . . .

. . . .

. . . .

. . . .

. . . .

impossible tricks 2

TODAY
you and your dog
WILL MASTER
another
IMPOSSIBLE
TRICK

Levitation

DAY 47

OUTSOURCE YOUR DOG'S JOBS: 2

STICK CHASING

Active canine sought for enthusiastic stick chasing in all weather.

SKILLS REQUIRED

- Very strong back legs
- Sensitive muzzle
- Boundless enthusiasm
- High tolerance of repetitive tasks
- Endless stores of energy

SHEPHERD

Wanted: Independent Ovine Production company, based in Wyoming, is looking for experienced, self-motivated Logistics Manager to work downline from Shep, our CEO, and traffic manager. Own crook and whistle required and references essential.

A WEEK FOR SPANIELS

Did you know that the first week in August is Spaniel Awareness week? Thought not.

OUTSOURCE YOUR DOG'S JOBS: 3

PEEING AGAINST LAMPPOSTS AND TREES

Uninhibited type needed for waste disposal and distribution program.

SKILLS REQUIRED

- Willing to deliver to organic and inorganic sites over a 24-hour period
- High-end directional skills
- Flexible bladder capacity

PHOTOSHOOT

Opportunity: Connecticut-based publisher invites dogs of all breeds and sizes to attend a photographic session; we need dogs to illustrate our exciting new book *This Book Will Change Your Dog's Life*. Must be willing to dress in ridiculous apparel and perform unusual tasks. Let us make you a star! Free chews and doggie treats.

POOCH POOLS!

Treat your dog to his own pool. Call toll-free

Deep Sea Dog

Introduce your dog to the rapture of the deep.

He will quickly learn to chase catfish. To avoid accidents, remember to take him outside before you put his wet-suit on.

Dog SWAP

Arrange a DOG SWAP with a dog from a DIFFERENT SOCIAL CLASS. Learn to become more tolerant of plebeian/patrician mores.

If the dog visiting you is of a higher social class, you may have to get used to fetching your own newspaper, though you should resist its efforts to usurp your position on the couch. If your visitor is a low-life, you should put a lock on the drinks cabinet and hide your monogrammed slippers.

Luscher color test day

On a large sheet of fabric pin eight pieces of card: violet, yellow, brown, gray, black, red, green, and blue. Watch your dog as he walks over them and note down the order he steps on them, especially the first and last card. Then look it up as a guide to your dog's inner character. Dress him in that color for the day to allow him to bond with it/experience its vibration.

■ Dog of god		■ Bipolar	
■ Happy		■ Pissed off	
■ Needs a poo		■ Jealous	
■ Boring (take him back to dog's home)		■ Contented (just eaten the cat)	

DAY 51

DAY 52

1 TODAY!

It is one year, in dog years, since you and your dog started on this project.

**Celebrate together
Make a cake**

HAPPY 1ST BIRTHDAY

ECODOG 2

REDUCE YOUR DOG'S CARBON PAW PRINT

There is no reason why your dog should not reduce his carbon paw print. Mix his turds with straw and bake into bricks in a slow oven or in the sun. Now build him a kennel out of his own waste matter, using his drool as a bonding agent(for more uses of drool, see day 18).

DAY 54

SACRIFICE

BE BRAVE.

Sacrifice your dog to the Jackal God Anubis. Lay his body under a cardboard pyramid overnight. By morning he should be restored to life.

YOUR DOG'S FAMILY TREE

Reawaken your dog's awareness of his roots by plotting his family tree. Write in the spaces provided, and help him stick in his family photos.

DAY 55

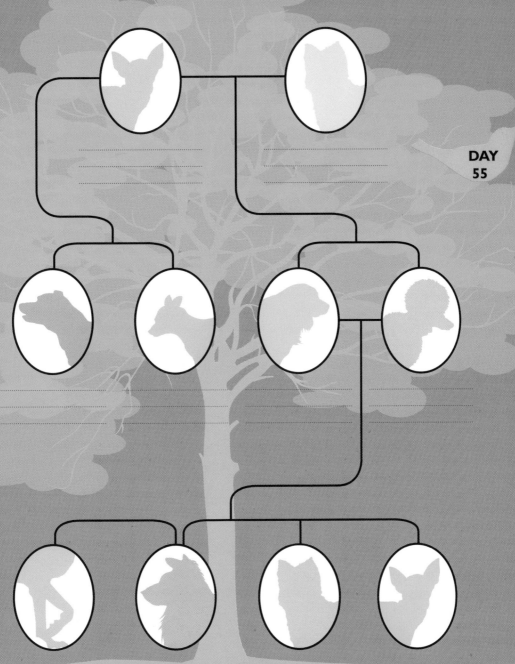

DAY 56

DOGGEREL

Cut up a poem into separate words.

Put it back together according to which words your dog chooses first.

Send to avant-garde poetry magazine.

sir dog

his

are whose

majesty's

I am pray

at

tell

Kew you?

me whose

dog

Degrees of Separation

Day 57

Work out how far your dog is away from fame by applying the six degrees test. For example:

1. Your dog.

2. Your neighbor's dog.

3. Your neighbor's cousin's dog in Omaha.

4. Your neighbor's cousin's dog's littermate in Denver.

5. Your neighbor's cousin's dog's littermate's owner's ex-husband in Paris, Texas.

6. Paris Hilton's dog.

You see how easy it is. Try it out on the bubble grid on the right.

4

5

3

Your Dog 1

2

6

DOG IN A MANGA

Exploit Your Dog ③

Aerial

Strap a small satellite dish to your back harness and put it on your dog. Train him to move about the room to pick up the optimum signal for your cell phone.

DAY 60

MAKING A BOW-WOW-LINE

Teach your dog how to **tie a bowline**, **using** a real **rabbit**, a real **hole**, and a real **tree**.

"The rabbit comes out of its hole, round the tree, and back down the hole again."

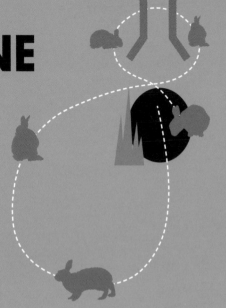

DAY 61

A DIFFERENT PERSPECTIVE

Why should your dog spend his whole life seeing and smelling things at one height? Make him some stilts* and take him for a walk to experience a whole new world.

* If your dog is very tall (Irish Wolfhound, Great Dane), train him to walk on his knees so he can see what life is like for ordinary dogs.

Six Bowls Theory

It was Edward de Bono (no relation) who introduced the concept of the Six Thinking Hats to decision-making and management models. Apply it to your dog, using bowls instead of hats. Present him with his food in a different colored bowl each day (white, black, blue, green, yellow, or red). Whichever bowl he favors indicates his basic nature.

White—pragmatic
It's chicken. A good source of protein. My amino acid quota will be filled today.

Red—passionate
I LOATHE chicken. It's disgusting, I'd rather tear out my own throat than eat this.

Black—negative
It's always chicken. She knows I hate chicken. God, I'm depressed.

Yellow—positive
Yippee! Chicken! Just as yummy as it was yesterday! How fantastic is that! Gimme more!

Green—creative
You know what, this chicken could be really something with a dash of tarragon vinegar.

Blue—controlling
Chicken again. Must track down the supplier and change the order.

*Put your dog's paw
print in the space above*

PaW
PaintinG

Help your dog express his artistic self;
provide paint and paper so that he can use
his paws (or maybe roll about a bit)
to produce a masterpiece. *Frame it.*

DAY 64

A Week of Linguistic Exploration: 1

This week, your dog will explore human expressions that can be taken literally and acted upon.

SCRAPE THE BARREL

* Purchase barrel.
* Smear with meat paste.
* Snap your dog scraping, for posterity.
* Try it inside the barrel.

DAY 65

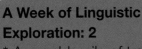

TAKE THE BISCUIT

A Week of Linguistic Exploration: 2

* Assemble pile of treats.
* Wait for your dog to take just one (it does not count if he takes more than one).

DAY 66

bark up the **wrong tree**

A Week of Linguistic Exploration: 3
* Go to a no-dogs area (at night if necessary).
* Find a tree.
* Encourage your dog to bark up into the canopy.

DAY 67

beat around the **bush**

A Week of Linguistic Exploration: 4
* Borrow another dog.
* Find a large bush.
* Set the dogs to chase each other around it.

chew
the fat

A Week of Linguistic Exploration: 5
* Purchase a slab of pork belly fat (lard is too soft to chew).
* Let your dog chew it.
* Time him.

bury the
hatchet

A Week of Linguistic Exploration: 6
* Get a hatchet.
* Rub with bonemeal.
* Place it within dog's view, handle foremost.
* See how long it takes him to bury it.

CARRY THE CAN

A Week of Linguistic Exploration: 7

* Select an empty can.
* Place it near your dog.
* Call him to heel, and reward him if he brings the can with him.

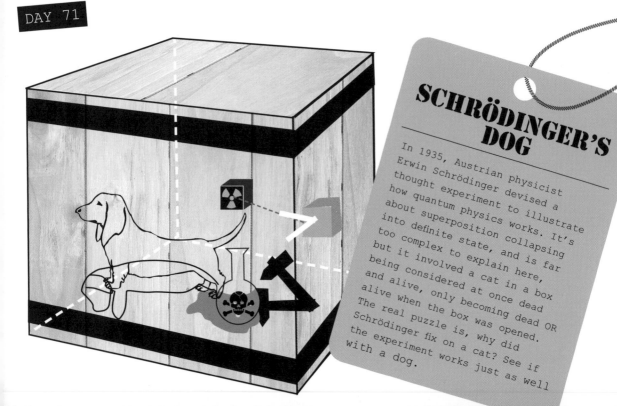

SCHRÖDINGER'S DOG

In 1935, Austrian physicist Erwin Schrödinger devised a thought experiment to illustrate how quantum physics works. It's about superposition collapsing into definite state, and is far too complex to explain here, but it involved a cat in a box being considered at once dead and alive, only becoming dead OR alive when the box was opened. The real puzzle is, why did Schrödinger fix on a cat? See if the experiment works just as well with a dog.

Confuse-a-Dog

Take your dog out for a game of catch and throw an orange (or grapefruit, depending on dog size) instead of a ball for him to catch.

???

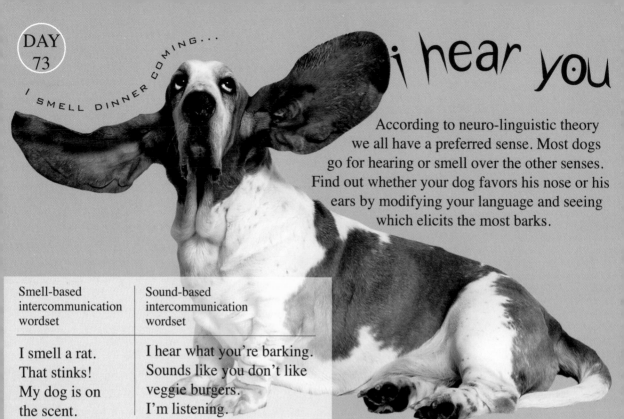

i hear you

According to neuro-linguistic theory we all have a preferred sense. Most dogs go for hearing or smell over the other senses. Find out whether your dog favors his nose or his ears by modifying your language and seeing which elicits the most barks.

Smell-based intercommunication wordset	Sound-based intercommunication wordset
I smell a rat. That stinks! My dog is on the scent.	I hear what you're barking. Sounds like you don't like veggie burgers. I'm listening.

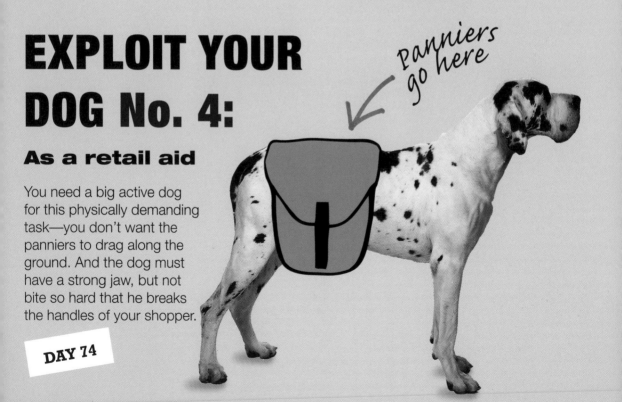

EXPLOIT YOUR DOG No. 4:

As a retail aid

You need a big active dog for this physically demanding task—you don't want the panniers to drag along the ground. And the dog must have a strong jaw, but not bite so hard that he breaks the handles of your shopper.

Panniers go here

DAY 74

Sky Dog

Arrange for your dog to perform a sponsored parachute jump for his favorite charity. This will improve his self-esteem and allow him to give something back to society. Don't tell him in advance though, in case his ethical commitment is not as well-developed as his cowardice.

DAY 76

Walk like an Egyptian

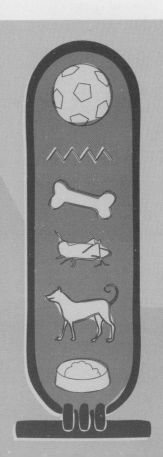

We know from Egyptian tombs that Egyptian dogs faced at right angles to the direction they were walking in. Today you will both do the same. If either of you falls in a ditch you fail the test and will be obliged to eat locusts (or similar).

FENG SHUI MY DOGHOUSE

The art of placement and decluttering can also enhance your dog's home. If he doesn't have a kennel, apply the technique to his basket, sofa, or favorite corner.

Opposite you will see a bagua compass, exactly as used for human feng shui but adapted for the canine consciousness.

Cut it out and line it up with the entrance to your dog's kennel or with the lower end of his basket. If all else fails, line it up with the north, then note the relevant areas.

On the right you will find some feng shui tips that will enhance the flow of chi for your dog.

Eight Feng Shui Tips

❶ Balance the Wood energy of the kennel with the Metal energy of your dog's bowl and the Water energy of the water in it.

❷ Tie red ribbons to his basket to prevent chi dissipating.

❸ Place black squeaky toys in his career corner.

❹ Pin a red rosette in his fame corner.

❺ Hang windchimes in the north corner of his kennel to get rid of stagnant sha (harmful energy).

❻ Place a purple dog chew in his prosperity corner.

❼ Soften the bad arrows of the kennel roof by placing round things, such as Frisbees, on each side.

❽ Avoid pink toys/treats in the marriage and partnership corner, unless you want puppies.

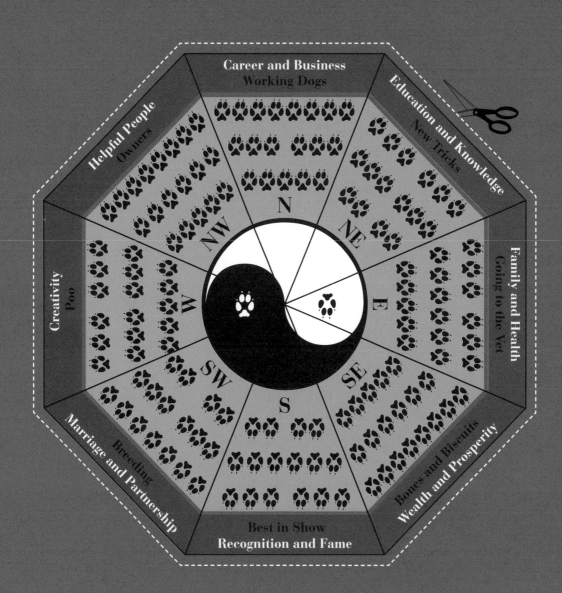

Re-Enacting History: 1
Sinking of the Titanic

You will need a boat and an iceberg. If your dog is small, use the bath, a model yacht, and ice cubes. You should sing and your dog should bark as the ship goes down.

Red Baron Day

Just because it's already been done by Snoopy as the Red Baron, don't think that your dog doesn't still want to do it. Think of it as homage. Hire a red bi-plane for the day, fit your dog out with flying goggles, and go out for a spin. It's best if one of you has a pilot's license.

THE WORLD IN A BASKET

Startle your dog out of his endemic speciesism. Take up a rainbow pet policy: adopt a cat, a newt, twin parrots, a family of gerbils, a stick insect, guppies, and a cormorant. Make space for them all in his kennel or basket.

DAY 80

DAY 81

GECKO FABULOUS

Cut out Velcro soles and stick them onto socks that will fit your dog snugly. Insert your dog's feet into the socks. Superglue trails of Velcro over your ceiling. Train your dog to walk along them.

DAY 82

VOILA!

SNIFFING BUTT

Today you will let your dog teach you HOW TO GREET FRIENDS in the canine manner.

RULES OF ENGAGEMENT

→ Go out for a walk.

→ When you see a friend, run toward him/her.

→ On reaching your friend, invade his/her social space and run around two or three times, wrapping the lead round his/her legs.

→ On the third circuit, get behind your friend. Bend down and ram your nose between his/her butt cheeks. Pant. Repeat.

→ Advanced work: when you have perfected this with people you already know, try it on strangers you like the look of.

Urinary Tracts

When the snow falls, allow your dog free expression. Photograph the pee trails and see if they make up words. Maybe your dog is trying to tell you something? Maybe he is the instrument of a random message from the universe? Maybe he has cystitis?

ECODOG 3

Farts

Harness your dog's farts to fuel your car. Set up the apparatus as shown in the diagram. Store harvested liquid methane in a safe container until you have enough. Here is a guide to yields over six months, sorted by breed:

1 wolfhound yields 20 gallons
1 terrier yields 10 gallons
1 dachshund yields 5 gallons
1 shih tzu yields 1 ½ pints

DOG YOGA

Yoga is very restful, apparently, so why not share it with your dog?

1. Do the Downward Facing Dog with him. This should be easy for him.

2. Follow it with the Stance of the Warrior. That should stop him acting so smug.

DAY 86

Divinity Day

Allow your dog to access his inner divinity by worshipping him for the day. Strew rose petals in his path and prostrate yourself before him. It's a useful exercise for honing your humility, too.

Turd Runes

Lacking in verbal skills, dogs have instead developed a complex excremental symbolism that can, to some degree, be learned by humans.

Finally, bluntness or sharpness of endpoint carries its own meaning.

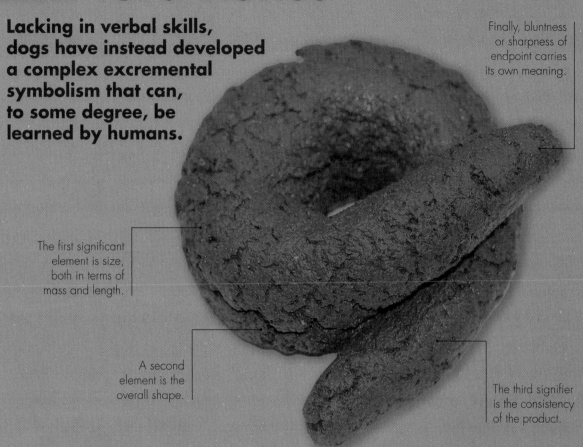

The first significant element is size, both in terms of mass and length.

A second element is the overall shape.

The third signifier is the consistency of the product.

	RABBIT DROPPINGS Small but perfectly formed, suggestive of taste and refinement.		**LOOSE AND LUMPY** A vulgar arrangement, indicative of too many dog chews.
	SINEWY 7 Rarely seen and usually an indicator of mystic powers in the turd creator.		**TERMITE MOUND** Precariously balanced, which suggests psychological instability and a cry for help.
	THEREFORE SIGN Shows a rational commitment to completing a job in manageable stages; very unusual.		**WHIPPY ICE CREAM** Perfectionism, sometimes taken to indicate a need to get out more.

DAY 88

A SCIENTIFIC EXPERIMENT

Apparently, chameleons change color in response to light exposure, ambient temperature, and whether they are feeling like cock-eyed optimists or the protagonist in a Russian play. They also change color to attract mates. We can find no research indicating that anybody has ever studied whether or not dogs change color under similar circumstances. Try it out now, you and your dog could be in for a Nobel.

1) Stretch your dog out on dpm* fabric.

2) Switch lights on and off at random.

3) Adjust heating and air conditioning.

4) Show him pictures of hot lady dogs.

Note down whether or not he starts to change color and match the background. Keep going for as long as you can, maybe time is a factor in canine chromomorphology.

dpm—military speak for dispersed pattern material, e.g. camo

DAY 89

DOGGIE DICTATORS

Let your dog access his inner dictator.
Use one of these handy instant dictator mustaches.

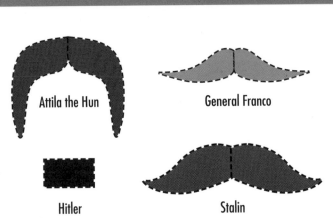

Attila the Hun

General Franco

Hitler

Stalin

WASTE SOME QUALITY TIME

DAY

See how long it takes to teach your dog to suck a mint with a hole down to nothing.

ENTER TIME HERE

DAY 91

❧ FIDO FIBONACCI ❧

For intellectual dogs: Teach your dog the Fibonacci sequence, using treats to get him to bark out the sequence from 0 to 89 (at least). The Fibonacci sequence describes, among other things, the arrangements of seeds in a sunflower head. That is why this dog is wearing a sunflower bonnet. It's both cute and intellectual.

After 0, 1, and 1, each number is the sum of the two preceding ones:

0	1	1	2	3	5	8	13	21	34
55	89	144	233	377	610	987	1597		
		2584	4181	6765					

Bark Code No.1

ワン,ワン!
WAN WAN

Foster global communication by teaching your dog to bark in various other languages. Today he can try Japanese, which is "wan-wan." When he gets good at it, teach him some doggy haikus—for example:

wan wan wan wan
wan wan wan
wan wan wan wan
wan wan wan wan wan wan

DAY 92

JAPANESE

DAY 93

RE-ENACTING HISTORY 2

Re-enact the Tet offensive; Put all your potted plants together to form a jungle in Vietnam. Dress your dog in a bandana in Rambo mode.

DOG NAM

DAY 94

TELEPATHY TRAINING

Concentrate on your dog and give him silent, mental commands, such as: Sit, lie down, bark, roll over, etc.

Keep a record of your dog's score and see how telepathic he is. If he's REALLY good at telepathy, try making it harder. Give him silent commands while he sleeps—for example, see if you can mentally make him twitch or wag his tail.

If he's hopeless at it, look on the bright side: At least you'll make him grateful for some spoken commands.

day 95

Absurdity Training 1

Subvert the habitual by training your dog to bark at every person he comes across who is wearing a hat.

DAY 96

Pointless Aggression

Pick a fight with a Rottweiler today. If your dog is already a Rottweiler, pick a fight with a Doberman.

Disrupt a Dog Show

Dog shows demean the entire canine species, emphasizing canine-unfriendly skills and encouraging selective breeding for features that please only humans, and often mean that dogs die young from avoidable conditions. It's gross exploitation of a largely disenfranchised societal group. Make a banner saying all this and disrupt your local dog show; when arrested take the opportunity to spread your message.

DAY 97

DAY 98

OUTSOURCE YOUR DOG'S JOBS: 4

HOWLING AT THE MOON

Flexi-time Lunar Regulation Engineer required to keep the moon in its rightful place.

SKILLS REQUIRED

- Excellent howling skills, ability to sustain long notes and project widely
- Good night vision
- Ability to work alone
- Willing to come out twice a month when required
- Ability to roll eyes an advantage
- No record of mental instability in the litter

HOUSEKEEPER

Required to head up domestic operations at Baskerville Hall. To oversee catering, laundry, and cleaning schedules, control the domestic budget, employ and regulate staff, and remain invisible to the hall owners and their relations and guests at all times unless required to answer questions posed by hawk-eyed independent investigating agents. A tolerance of dogs and phosphorous is essential.

IDITAROD RUNNERS

Why not sign up to Iditarod Reunited, the great new site for huskies and sled dogs

DAY 99
TRANSCENDENTAL HOWLING

om

🐾 Set aside half an hour every evening when the moon rises for meditative howling to help your dog balance his chakras and center himself.

🐾 Offer him a saffron-colored rug to sit on.

🐾 Encourage him to howl on one note (om). Join in if you can.

🐾 On moonless nights just stare at your navels. This may be easier for him than for you.

DAY 100

SPIRITUAL LEANINGS 1

You have no idea what religion or spiritual system your dog subscribes to. **MAYBE HE IS A DRUID.** To find out:

- 🐾 Nail a sprig of mistletoe to his kennel.
- 🐾 Present his biscuit in the shape of a henge.
- 🐾 Make him a coronet of oak leaves.
- 🐾 Host a druid cultural festival in your backyard.

DAY 101

DOG HEAVEN

Your dog is a good dog. Treat him to a day in heaven to show what delights await him.

While he sleeps, drape the whole room in white. Replace his basket, toys, and bowl with white versions and feed him minced chicken breast and pale bones.

Make a halo out of an old Frisbee and some wings out of wire and gauze. Play all his favorite games and let him sleep on the couch.

DAY 102

REVERSE PAVLOV

Indulge your dog, and let him play reverse Pavlov to your salivating hound. Whenever he barks, you drink a martini cocktail.* (You will have to have them ready mixed and strategically placed around the house, plus a hipflask for walks). Note how long it takes for you to start salivating whenever he barks.

*Or your drink of choice

DAY 103

WALTER MUTTY

Your dog has a rich inner life you know nothing about. He may have heroic daydreams and wild adventures. Concentrate and see if you can access his inner spiderman.

DAY 104

2 TODAY!

It is two years, in dog years, since you and your dog started on this project.

**Celebrate together
Make a cake
Give a gift**

HAPPY 2ND BIRTHDAY

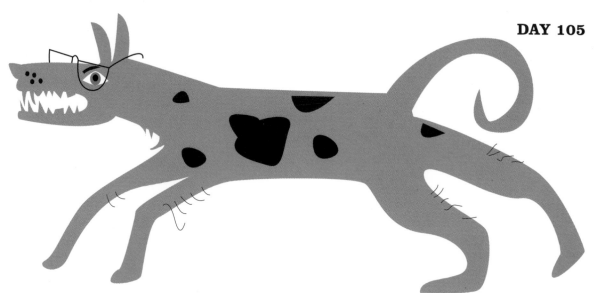

TOP DOG

If your dog is getting uppity, hire a dog costume of a bigger, fiercer dog. Wear it around the house to show him who's boss.

NEVER MIND THE DOG'S BOLLOCKS

Access your dog's inner punk. Give him a Ramones T-shirt to distress before putting it on him. Add a spiked or studded collar and some bondage chains for his back legs. Play music by the Sex Pistols, the Ramones, Iggy and the Stooges, the Clash, the Slits, etc. Encourage him to jump about a lot, and let him spit and drool as much as he wants.

NOW THAT'S WHAT I CALL . . .

Lighten your dog's mood by compiling a CD or an MP3 collection of dog-inspired songs from all genres. If he likes it, market it via his website and split the proceeds.

DOG SONGS

Who Let the Dogs Out? *Baha Men*

How Much Is That Doggie in the Window? *Patti Page*

Puppy Love *Donny Osmond*

Slap My Bitch Up *The Prodigy*

He's a Tramp *Peggy Lee*

Doggy Dogg World *Snoop Dogg*

Pet Sounds *The Beach Boys*

Me and You and a Dog Named Boo *Lobo*

I Love My Dog *Cat Stevens*

Werewolves of London *Warren Zevon*

Hounds of Love *Kate Bush* or *The Futureheads*

Diamond Dogs *David Bowie*

DAY 108

BONE VOUCHERS

Encourage good behavior. Your dog gets a voucher for each bad habit that he avoids. Two vouchers in a day gets a bone. Four vouchers gets a T-bone. Six vouchers gets a weekend with Madonna's dog.

no drinking from the lavatory

no bottom wiping on carpet

no humping every visitor

no Brussels sprout farts

no butt sniffing

no nighttime yowling

DAY 109
SUPERPOOCH

Does your dog have superpowers? How will you know unless you dress him in a ridiculous costume, throw him into a situation of mortal danger, and see how he gets out of it? Do it today!

This can be done indoors or outdoors. The idea is to get around the room/apartment/block/park touching the ground as little as possible and using items of furniture, urban architecture, or natural features to bounce off. If your dog is not doing so well, hire a cat as a trainer.

DAY 111

ROB A BANK

Observe your local bank.
No one will question someone hanging around while their dog sniffs hydrants. When you have enough information, go home and plan the heist.

Train your dog to growl like a Doberman (unless he is a Doberman). Knit balaclavas for yourself and your dog. Wear gloves and put socks on all four dog feet. Do the job, with you as gang leader and dog as bagman. He will run home and bury the stash. You go in the opposite direction. Reassemble when coast is clear.
Move to Acapulco

WAXWORK

Make a waxwork of your dog. Dress it in your dog's leash and collar and stand it near its basket. See how long it takes for your real dog to get into a howling rage of jealousy.

DAY 113

ONLINE FUN

Sign your dog up to World of Warcraft. Let him choose to be Alliance or Horde by drawing the short dog chew for Alliance or the long one for Horde. (Hold a bunch of chews, one chopped in half) and let him select.) Only allow him to play for an hour each day; what? you want an MMORPG* nerd for a pet?

*A massive multiplayer online role-playing game

HANDY CAT IDENTIFIER

Cats can be tricky, and don't look the same head on as they do from a side view. Here is a handy guide.

| Side View of Cat | Cat in a Tree | Spiteful Cat | Stalking Cat | Rolling Cat |

| Playful Cat | Sleeping Cat | Pouncing Cat | Hunter Cat | Front View of Cat |

DAY 115

impossible trick 3

Today, you and your dog will master another impossible trick.

transmuting dog cookies into gold

OUTSOURCE YOUR DOG'S JOBS: 5

CAT CHASING

Fit young Feline Harassment Officer required for shift work. Must be a very fast worker.

DAY 116

SKILLS REQUIRED

- ■ 0–25 mph in 3 seconds
- ■ No fear of trees
- ■ Ability to judge the size of small gaps
- ■ Excellent night vision
- ■ Thick-haired breeds will have an obvious advantage
- ■ Willing to work in a group

CHAIR TESTER

Wanted: Excessively idle volunteer needed to test comfort quotient of chair seats. Suit single cat.

DAY 117

Road Runner

Let your dog drive for the day.

This works only if you drive an automatic

subvert the system

Enter your dog in a show* in the wrong class. Insist that he is the correct breed/gender despite clear evidence to the contrary. If refused, sue on the basis of workplace discrimination.

* For a more confrontational and life-changing experience, enter him in a cat show.

Sensory Deprivation Day

This is good for your dog.

Dog Stars 1

Your dog will be thrilled to discover that his species is mirrored in the heavens. Teach him to recognize the dog-themed constellations and bark at them as they come up over the eastern horizon.

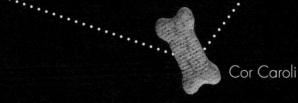

Star cluster

Canes Venatici is a northern sky constellation. It represents Chara and Asterion, the two hunting dogs of Boötes. The alpha star is Cor Caroli.

Cor Caroli

CANES VENATICI

Day for Night

Baffle your dog by swapping day for night. Give him breakfast at 9:00 in the evening, take him out for a long walk by moonlight, paint his toys with luminous paint so he can play with them in the dark. Give him dinner at 6:00 in the morning, lock the door, and go to bed.

DAY 122

FETCH A FORTUNE

Buy 49 rubber bone-type chews. WRITE NUMBERS 1–49 on them. Get your DOG to FETCH six chews at random. Use the numbers for the LOTTERY.

DAY 123

FINANCIAL ADVICE

For **super-rich dogs** who get **left all** of their owner's **inheritance (and how to spend it)**

Last Will a
To my beloved Dog
to spend on luxury
opulence and ple
the mega sum of

Things to do

Hire security guards. Now that you are a dog of property there will be plenty of people taking an interest in you.

Take out a pension plan. Just because you are OK now doesn't mean you shouldn't plan for old age, which arrives pretty quickly when you are a dog.

Go on a cruise, but watch out for gold-diggers.

Move to Florence in Italy. Dogs are allowed in almost everywhere in Florence except the Opera House.

Make a will. You can't take it with you.

DAY 124

CANINE CREDIT

APPLY FOR A CREDIT CARD IN YOUR DOG'S NAME. MAX IT OUT. FILE HIM FOR BANKRUPTCY.

NOTHING WILL HAPPEN BECAUSE IT IS ILLEGAL TO GIVE A DOG A CREDIT CARD.

DAY 125

DOUBLE INDEMNITY

INSURE YOUR DOG'S TAIL
Trap it in a door.
Make the claim and
SPLIT THE PROCEEDS.

DAY 126 NETWORKING

WHEN did your DOG last make a NEW FRIEND?

It is your **duty** today to introduce him to:

- ☐ 1 Labrador
- ☐ 1 St. Bernard
- ☐ 1 Poodle
- ☐ 1 Chihuahua

(tick when mission accomplished)

RULES OF ENGAGEMENT

- 🐾 Each dog must be a different breed from your dog.
- 🐾 If this isn't the case, substitute the relevant duplicate with a schnauzer.
- 🐾 Meetings must be spontaneous.
- 🐾 You may help with identification, but your dog must make the first move.
- 🐾 If target dog is smaller, go in humble.
- 🐾 If target dog is bigger, go in dominant.
- 🐾 No biting.

new friend

Name ....

Tel. no.......................

Meeting place ....

....

First impressions ....

....

....

Friendability rating ....
from 1–10

new friend

Name ....

Tel. no.......................

Meeting place ....

....

First impressions ....

....

....

Friendability rating ....
from 1–10

new friend

Name ....

Tel. no.......................

Meeting place ....

....

First impressions ....

....

....

Friendability rating ....
from 1–10

new friend

Name ....

Tel no ....

Meeting place ....

....

First impressions ....

....

....

Friendability rating ....
from 1–10

*Color in the drawings to make them look like your dog's new friends

WHICH CAR?

A CANINE GUIDE TO THE TOP 10 CARS

- Buick station wagon—plenty of room in the back.
- 4 x 4—hard to climb into unless you are a Great Dane.
- Honda Civic—cramped and often smells of old lady.
- Lexus—very swish but you won't be allowed in it.
- Toyota Prius—might as well walk.
- VW Beetle—Afghans only.
- Alfa Romeo Spyder—great if you like the wind in your hair.
- Hummer—for the macho types.
- Stretch limo—good for parties or if you belong to a family of dachshunds.
- Citroën 2CV—makes a nice kennel.

DAY 128

SELL ADVERTISING SPACE

ON YOUR DOG TO LOCAL BUSINESSES.

HARRY'S HOT DOGS

Exhibit Your Dog

Trafalgar Square in London, England, has an empty plinth that artists take in turns to fill with their oeuvre. Why not apply to have your dog standing there for a few days? Make a caption to stand with him—for example, Fortitude, Dog Number 41, The Dog Descending the Staircase, Opus 6, Still-Life with Bowl, Flea Field, etc.

If you do not live in a city that has this facility, petition for one.

DAY 129

DOG ICONS
The Top Dogs

Laika
The first dog in space
In 1957, Laika (née Kudryavka) became not only the first dog, but the first living being in space.

Strongheart
The first dog movie star
Etzel von Oeringen (1917–29) was born in Germany but made it big in the USA in White Fang (1925).

Toby
The first dog millionaire
In 1932, Ella Wendal left 75 million dollars to her Standard Poodle called Toby.

Laddie Boy
The first First Dog
Warren G. Harding (president 1921–3) set the precedent for First Dog with his beloved Airedale terrier.

Stubby
The first war dog
After serving at the front for 18 months in World War I, Stubby was decorated by General Pershing.

Moose
The world's heaviest dog
The English Mastiff from New Jersey weighed in at 291 lbs in 2001.

Bluey
The world's oldest dog
The cattle dog from Victoria lived to the age of 29, from June 1910 to November 1939.

Buddy
The first seeing eye dog
Buddy, a German Shepherd, became the guide dog for Morris Frank in 1928.

Be Inspired

Despite being canine, many dogs have burst through the species ceiling and become bona fide firsts. Why can't your dog? Encourage him to smarten up, get his butt in gear, and start thinking outside the basket and make something of himself.

Dress the part. It's all about image, so get him measured up for a custom-made suit.

Cultivate a sincere look and untroubled brow; he is confident, poised, and ready for anything.

Look all business with a fat bag of papers and important stuff.

Always be open-handed; it shows generosity of spirit and a willingness to engage with the world.

Vital parts exposed shows you have the nads for the job and saves time later when you and the secretary are back in the office.

Build a Doggy Library

Buy these books in the thrift store. Put them in your dog's kennel or on a small shelf by your dog's basket. See which one he eats first.

DAY 131

THE CURIOUS INCIDENT of the DOG IN THE NIGHT-TIME
MARK HADDON

DOG YEARS
GUNTHER GRASS

The Day of the Jackal
Frederick Forsyth

DAY 132

SIT! STAY! READ!

TEACH YOUR DOG TO READ

Use simple sentences on flash cards in front of your dog's food bowl, for reward.

Dogs in Literature

Hound of the Baskervilles (Sir Arthur Conan Doyle) **Call of the Wild** (Jack London) **White Fang** (Jack London) **Old Yeller** (Fred Gipson) **Three Men in a Boat: To Say Nothing of the Dog** (Jerome K. Jerome) **Black Dogs** (Ian McEwan) **Spy Dog** (Andrew Cope) **The Power of the Dog** (Don Winslow) **The Terracotta Dog** (Andrea Camilleri) **Black Dog** (Stephen Booth) **The Finer Points of Sausage Dogs (Portuguese Irregular Verbs)** (Alexander McCall Smith) **Red Dog** (Louis De Bernières) **Wolves Eat Dogs** (Martin Cruz Smith) **Anarchy and Old Dogs** (Colin Cotterill) **Dog Eats Dog** (Iain Levison) **The Dogs of War** (Frederick Forsyth) **The Yellow Dog** (Georges Simenon) **Greyfriars Bobby** (Eleanor Atkinson) **The Curious Incident of the Dog in the Night-Time** (Mark Haddon) **Dogger** (Shirley Hughes) **The Lady with the Little Dog** (Anton Chekhov) **The Day of the Jackal** (Frederick Forsyth) **The Dogs of Riga** (Henning Mankell and Laurie Thompson)

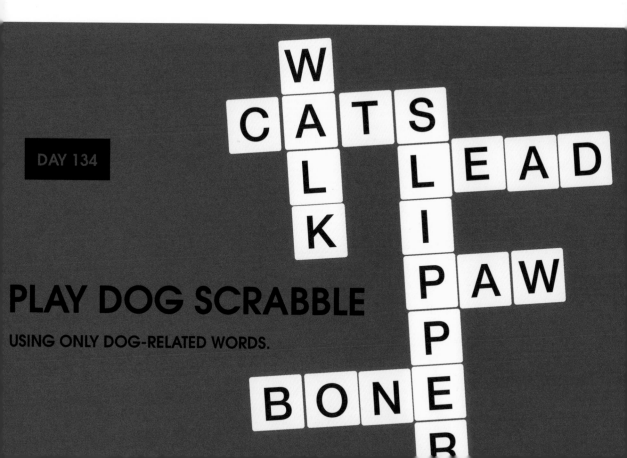

DAY 134

PLAY DOG SCRABBLE

USING ONLY DOG-RELATED WORDS.

TOUGH LOVE

Leave your dog in a dog's home for the day. Teach him to appreciate what he has got.

DAY 135

BE MEAN TO YOUR DOG

Tired of your dachshund? Fed up with that doleful look, the fact that it takes hours to walk anywhere, and that dachshunds are always in paintings with rich-looking women? Why not take him down to the nearest hot dog stand and swap him for the real thing? Think about it …

DAY 136

DAY 137

SELF-REFLECTION
—DAY—

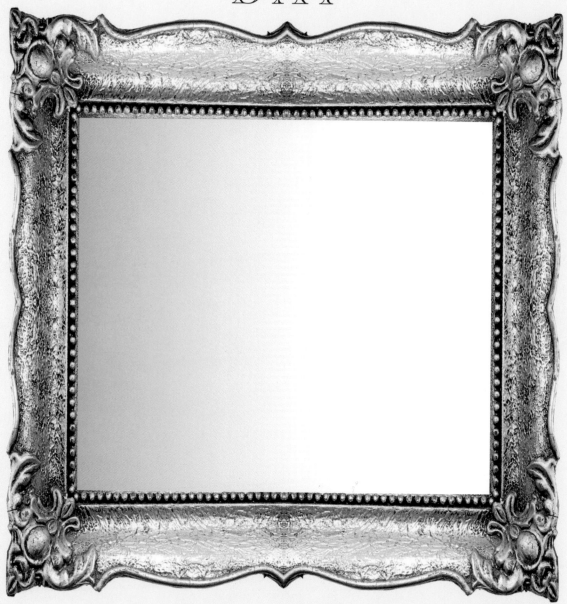

Stand your dog in front of the largest mirror you own. Give the command "STAY" and let him reflect on himself for the day.

DAY 138

Masterclass 4

LEG HUMPING

Today you will let your dog teach you HOW TO GET RID OF EXCESS SEXUAL ENERGY.

RULES OF CONTACT

OUTDOORS

→ 1. Go for a walk.

→ 2. When your dog stops to greet a friend, walk round the owner, sniffing appreciatively.

→ 3. Hunker down and clamp your arms and knees around whichever leg is easiest to reach.

→ 4. Perform rhythmic pelvic thrusts. You can whine while you are doing it.

→ Variant: If you are shy, or unsure of your technique, you practice on a tree trunk or large furniture until you feel confident enough to go live.

INDOORS

→ 1. Wait for visitors to arrive, preferably a friend with someone else you don't know.

→ 2. Perform steps 2-4 (see Outdoors, left).

CENSORED

DAY 139

- Obtain phosphorus
- Apply to dog
- Try to scare neighbor to death

Hound of the Baskervilles

DAY 140

SELLING UP

SOLD

Put your dog, his bowls, toys, leash, basket, and bones on eBay. Buy a new dog with the money.

DAY 141

ONE DOG LEG

Embarrass your dog today.

Hop everywhere when you take him for a walk.

DAY 142

DANGEROUS DRESSING

PIMP YOUR DOG AND YOURSELF IN MATCHING PINK AND VISIT YOUR LEAST FAVORITE NEIGHBOR. TU TU, TIARA, AND BOWS ALL REQUIRED.

DAY 143

Designer
CROSS BREEDING

Make the next designer dog

Cut out pictures from magazines and lay them together to make your own designer dog. Look out for any improvements to the real thing lying asleep in the corner.

INTRODUCING THE CREMATIHAN

CHINESE CRESTED HEAD

Eye-catching headgear; dramatic without being ostentatious.

DALMATION BODY

A touch of the Cruellas always makes a statement.

Remember not to mix spots with stripes.

AFGHAN HOUND FEET

Furry boots are a little Nicole Richie for some tastes, but they show that you are worth it.

DAY 144

KING/QUEEN FOR A DAY

MAKE YOUR DOG FEEL ROYAL

MAKE a crown, throne, golden food bowls, stamps, coat of arms, basket with royal arms on, gilded toys, etc.

GENDER REASSIGNMENT DAY

Since your dog is probably not what he was when born, let him try out a different gender for a day. He might like it. If your dog is entire, it will challenge his stereotypical notions.

TIPS

* Call your dog by a feminized/masculinized version of his/her name, e.g. Fido/Felicity, Bonzo/Bonza, Wilkins/Mrs. Wilkins.

* Don't let your male dog cock his leg; don't let your female dog squat.

* Color-code leashes, bowls, and blankets to suit gender expectation.

Be Prepared

Splint your dog's back legs so that he can prepare mentally for old age.

Day 146

DAY 147

DISGUISE A DOG

Baffle your friends by **disguising your dog as:**

racula

A clown

A dinosaur

DAY 148

MAKEOVER

WHEN did you last visit the poodle parlor?

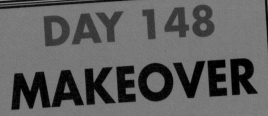

WHO'S THE DOG?

Choose today from the following styles:

HRH style: QUEEN FOR A DAY
Get a blue rinse to go with your blue blood.

Appointment Card

Salon ....

Tel. no. ....

Appointments ....

....

....

....

....

....

....

....

....

70s style: KING OF COOL
Never a poodle but a 20th-century dog!

Icon style: HOLLYWOOD HOT
A buxom blonde always has more fun!

Go figure style: MAD DOG MOHICAN
Who's the dog? You're the dog …

茶式 style: GEISHA TEA COSY
When a life needs a little more ceremony …

Masterclass 5

Today you will let your dog teach you how to beg.

1. Go to the bar with your dog.
2. Get down on all fours.
3. Look up at the bartender and cock your head to one side, looking winsome.
4. Stare fixedly at the vodka bottle*.
5. Whine pathetically.
6. Whenever the bartender goes near the bottle, pump up the whining, and rise up on your knees, holding your hands in front of you.
7. Pant.

When you get the drink, slug it down in one, then wag your butt, and pant some more.

or bourbon bottle, or beer pump, or cocktail shaker.

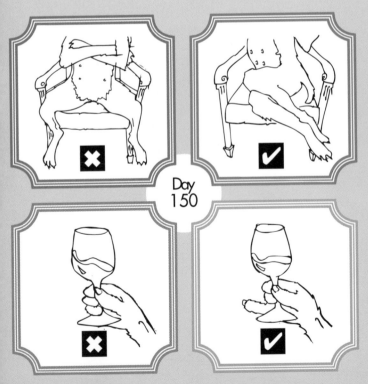

Day 150

Finishing School

Your dog may be trained but is he refined? Set up your own finishing school to transform him into a confident, polished canine, at home anywhere from Miami to the Hamptons.

✳ Deportment classes—to teach your dog to walk elegantly around a room balancing a Breed Guide book on his head.

✳ Received barking—to teach him that one bark, delivered with authority but in a pleasing register, gets more attention than 20 minutes of frenzied yapping.

✳ Bone etiquette—to help him choose which part of dinner to eat first, and how to chew bones from the left only.

✳ Elegance—to teach your dog the best way to get out of his basket or off the rug.

day 151

Give your dog a virtual foreign holiday

Your dog would like to be a world citizen, but neither of you can cope with all that long-haul travel (especially not in the hold).

Simply photograph him and place him against a scanned backdrop of the world's great tourist destinations—the Tour Eiffel, the Taj Mahal, Buckingham Palace, Mt. Fuji.

VACATION DESTINATIONS TO AVOID—CHINA

Reasons NOT to go

Especially if you are a St. Bernard

- Some dog breeds are popular as a meat dish; they are more expensive than pork and usually cooked for special occasions or feasts.
- Some Chinese men believe that eating dogmeat (along with snake soup) will enhance their sexual stamina.
- St. Bernards are particularly highly regarded.

HOLA

POST CARD

YOU GOT MAIL

Your dog gets no mail. What does this do for his self-esteem? Whenever you go out, mail him postcards of exotic locations (or the mall, he won't know) so that he feels part of your life. If you want to show off, write a message in a language he doesn't know.

O. Shep

2140 Main Street

Berkeley

CA 94707

DAY 153

Bark Code No.2

WANG WANG

If your dog has mastered Japanese (see Day 90), Chinese barking should be a walk in the park. Mandarin Chinese dogs say "wang wang," pronounced "wong wong." This works for Taiwan as well, and may well be very useful over the next decade or so when China becomes the new world power.

DAY 154

CHINESE

DAY 155

VACATION DESTINATIONS TO AVOID—NIGERIA

Where DOG is on the MENU

Eating Dog is ingrained in Nigerian culture.

They believe:
- 🐾 It offers protection against witchcraft.
- 🐾 It can be used as a cure against malaria.
- 🐾 It improves your sex life.
- 🐾 It helps prevent poison from killing a person.

DAY 156

3 TODAY!

It is three years, in dog years, since you and your dog started on this project.

Celebrate together
Make a cake
Give a gift
Send a card

HAPPY 3RD BIRTHDAY

A TEST OF TRUST

Using numbers taken from your dog's birthday, weight, age, and name expressed numerologically (see right), choose a horse race and place each way bets. Promise to spend all the money on him if the horses win.

WORKING OUT YOUR DOG'S NAME IN NUMBERS

If your dog is called Bonzo, his number will be

B=2 +O=6 +N=5 +Z=8 + O=6

This makes 27, or 9 when reduced to one digit (2+7=9).

A1	B2	C3	D4
E5	F6	G7	H8
I9	J1	K2	L3
M4	N5	O6	P7
Q8	R9	S1	T2
U3	V4	W5	X6
Y7	Z8		

Ecodog 4

Harness your dog's natural energy and use him to power all or part of your home. If he is seriously energetic, you may be able to make a small profit selling back surplus energy to the grid.

1. Measure your dog and build or purchase a treadmill to fit.
2. Look on the Internet and find out how to build a device that will convert the energy generated when he runs on the treadmill into a form that can be stored in battery cells OR routed directly into a generator.
3. Set him running.

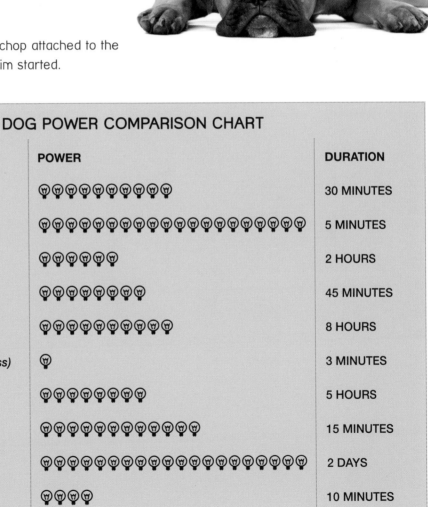

TIP: A sausage or a pork chop attached to the treadmill is useful to get him started.

DOG POWER COMPARISON CHART

DOG TYPE	POWER	DURATION
1 ST BERNARD	💡💡💡💡💡💡💡💡💡	30 MINUTES
1 GREYHOUND	💡💡💡💡💡💡💡💡💡💡💡💡💡💡💡💡💡💡	5 MINUTES
1 TERRIER	💡💡💡💡💡💡	2 HOURS
1 COLLIE	💡💡💡💡💡💡💡	45 MINUTES
1 HUSKY	💡💡💡💡💡💡💡💡💡	8 HOURS
3 CHIHUAHAUS (in harness)	💡	3 MINUTES
1 POODLE	💡💡💡💡💡💡💡	5 HOURS
1 LURCHER	💡💡💡💡💡💡💡💡💡💡	15 MINUTES
1 GREAT DANE	💡💡💡💡💡💡💡💡💡💡💡💡💡💡💡💡💡	2 DAYS
1 BULLDOG	💡💡💡💡	10 MINUTES

DAY 159

Art Class 1

Apart from a few noble exceptions, dogs never really star in great paintings of the world, and your dog may not fully appreciate the old masters because they do not reflect his image. Change this by combining a cut-up photo of your dog with a postcard of a great work. Here you see the Mona Lisa, or La Giochounda. Ha ha.

La Giaconda (Mona Lisa), 1503–19, Leonardo da Vinci

DAY 160

DOODLE
YOUR STANDING
POODLE 1

Doodle your poodle* standing up (the dog, not you). We have given you feet and head for starters, now it's up to you. Relax the wrist and stare at your dog until you are in a trance-like state so that doodling comes easy.

*You can also doodle other breeds.

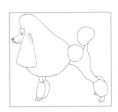

All things dogs love to do, in outline for you to color in.

COLOR-IN FUN

DOGS LOVE...

...sniffing butt

...bones

...chewy and squeaky toys

...anything tall and upright for shooting practice

...food, and eating

...hogging the sofa

A Bar at the Folies Bergères, 1882, Edouard Manet

ART CLASS 2

MAYBE YOUR DOG WOULD PREFER HIS ART MORE NINE-TEENTH CENTURY? A BIT MORE BOHÈME? WHY NOT TRY OUT "A BAR(K) AT THE FOLIES BERGÈRES." FRAME THE RESULT TO GIVE A BETTER IMPRESSION.

DAY 163

DOODLE
YOUR RUNNING
POODLE 2

Doodle your poodle in motion. This is much more of a challenge than plain old doodling (see Day 160) and may require you to move with him (try in-line skates, more stable than a bicycle for doodling purposes).

GET DOODLING

DAY 164

DOODLE
YOUR SITTING
POODLE 3

Doodle your poodle sitting down. We have provided a head, front foot and back foot to get you started, now it's up to you. Don't obsess with accuracy, just try to capture the pose. This is also an excellent opportunity to train your dog to sit still for long periods.

GET DOODLING

DAY 165
Art Class 3

**Hans Holbein the Younger;
Henry VIII; 1539-40**

This is great for small dogs or dogs with low self-esteem; seeing himself as England's most powerful monarch in a big frock will do wonders for his amour propre.

JOIN THE DOTS

Is it a cat? Is it a squirrel? Starting at 1, help your dog to join the dots together until an exciting chase-object is revealed.

start

DAY 167

Art Class 4

The Marriage of the Giovanni Arnolfini and Giovanna Cenami, 1434, Jan van Eyck

The famous Arnolfini Marriage would be a good choice for the homeloving dog; it's a classic of its genre and especially useful if you are trying to mate your hound and produce a new revenue stream of delightful puppies.

CANINE HYDROMANCY

Predict the future by the patterns made when your dog shakes himself after a bath or a swim.

SPATTER MARKS GROUPED CLOSELY TOGETHER

This signifies a gathering. Could be good (your friends are throwing you a surprise party) or not so good (all your family—including Insane Uncle Kenneth the Alabama Arsonist—are coming for Thanksgiving).

SPATTER MARKS IN A CIRCLE

This is very auspicious: Round equates with fullness and coins. Expect a windfall or a bonus, or at least to find a couple of bucks down the back of the couch.

SPATTER MARKS VERY SPARSE AND FAR WAY FROM EACH OTHER

Presages a soul-sapping week or so under the heavy arm of bureaucracy, probably the Internal Revenue Service. Get your dog to deal with the paperwork. It will be just as wrong, but not nearly so stressful for you.

SPATTER MARKS IN STRAIGHT LINE

This is a good sign only if you are looking for a quiet life, because it indicates that the next four weeks are going to be models of routine and repetition unrelieved by any spontaneity or fun.

Sultan Poklington Winstanley-Witherspoon III
of Clarksville ("Pongo")
The Old Kennels
16 Doberman Street
Boston
MA 02110

8472183

REDISCOVERING ANCESTORS

This is the day to help your dog rediscover his heritage and reconnect with his ancestors. Draw his family tree, and show it to him. Restore ritual into his life by performing a naming ceremony for him as the next heir to his doggie line, then dedicate some foods, e.g. marrow bones, dog treats, hamburger, cheese. Let the foods stand for an hour, then let him eat them.

DAY 169

RE-ENACTING HISTORY 3

Battle of Little Big Horn

Re-enact the famous and heroic last stand of General Custer and his 7th Cavalry in 1876. You, and anyone else (including any dogs) who wants to take part, are the Lakota-Cheyenne Alliance, and your dog is Custer. If he runs away when you start throwing toothpicks at him, it will prove that dogs are smarter than humans.

DAY 170

DAY 171

TIME MACHINE

Fool your dog into thinking you have a time machine. Decorate a box with lights and knobs. Put him in it and play Van Halen very loud. While he is there, bring out the younger dog you have secretly borrowed, hired, or bought. Tell him that it is his younger self and that he has transgressed the temporal laws and now the fabric of the universe is split.

Cagney and Lassie

Set up a private detective agency with your dog. He can hang around unobtrusively outside the love nests of philandering husbands while you sit in the car with your collar turned up, chewing a matchstick. If your dog isn't the unobtrusive type he can chew the matchstick and you'll have to do the hanging around.

DAY 173

Pizza Pooch

Go to the pizza parlor where they advertise any topping you like. Ask for a Four Seasons for your dog with chopped liver, sausage, T- bone steak, and dog treats*. Salad is optional, but no banana split unless he finishes, and definitely no garlic bread (unless you have a spinone).

* Ask for a doggy bag if he doesn't finish.

Ecodog 5

Day 174

Make a rainstick for your dog to fetch.

1. Trim your dog's toenails.
2. Collect clippings.
3. Pour into a long, thin tube that can be sealed.
4. Seal the tube.
5. Rotate the rainstick so your dog can hear the clippings trickle.
6. Wait for it to rain.

NEIGHBORHOOD ·GUARD·

Send your dog round to guard your neighbor's house for a change.

DAY 175

Re-Enacting History 4:
The Boston Tea Party

Re-enact one of the iconic moments of US history with your dog, using only the dog's bath, some packets of loose tea, and a musket-shaped water gun.

Make Your Dog Feel Inferior 2

DAY 177

Research and find a shot of the Amundsen Expedition to the South Pole. Roald Amundsen and his team of five took four sledges and 52 dogs and set off on October 19, 1911. They arrived at the Pole on December 14. Photoshop your idle hound into the shot and show it to him when he starts getting uppity about walking in cold weather.

PRESIDENT DOG

TO BECOME PRESIDENT, YOUR DOG:

Must be at least five years old (35 human years) and be born in the USA, Guam, Puerto Rico, or the US Virgin Islands, or descended from American dogs living abroad. Needs to have been a US resident for at least two years.

Try to find father, check out nationality

Should have a law degree (get one online) and/or done some government service. Governors, 15 senators, and 19 members of the House of Representatives have all become president in this way.

check on eBay

Raise money; he will need around $200 million.

Savings=$14 so need to tighten belt

Appoint a devoted campaign team.

Name a running mate, someone not quite as cute but good at what you're not, maybe a sniffer dog who is hot on law and order.

See if either Bill Clinton's or George Bush's dogs are still around—they are sure to be good at manipulating the law and be able to sniff an easy college intern at 50 paces

Lobby other dogs.

Don't let Bill's dog get anyone in the lobby

Win 270 electoral college votes.

Learn to bark the inaugural oath "I do solemnly swear (or affirm) that I will faithfully execute the office of president of the United States, and will to the best of my ability preserve, protect, and defend the constitution of the United States."

Woof, woof... well it's a start

Binary Barking

Teach your dog to interface directly with your computer to save all that tedious keying. He will need to learn binary code; fortunately this is easy (see right). Then all you have to do is show him print-outs of the necessary coding.

0= 0 bark

1= 1 bark

Extreme sports 2: Free-falling

This is when you jump out of an airplane with a parachute but don't open it until you are very near the ground. Apparently the adrenaline rush is unbeatable. Make sure your dog can pull the chute toggle before you let him take any solo falls.

DAY 181

Today you will give up chasing cars and your dog will give up smoking.

Self-Denial Day

Self-Denial Day II

DAY 182

Right. This time you will do it properly. You will give up soduku and your dog will give up leg-humping. See who cracks first.

DAY 183
ELEVATE THE TONE

If your dog has been good, give him a treat by providing him with some great art that reflects his species and breed. Purchase art posters of paintings of dogs by great masters, and hang them by his basket. This foxhound, called Ringwood, is by George Stubbs and belonged to the Earl of Yarborough. How elevated do you want to get?

DAY 184

MAKE THE WORLD GO AWAY

Send your dog on retreat to a monastery, preferably one run by the Franciscan Order.

Repurpose Your Dog 1
Reflexologist

Reflexology is expensive, and it's not nice having strangers tickle your tootsies. Why not let your Old Faithful do the job? Obtain one of those foot maps reflexologists use, lay down, and let your dog lick your soles. Take your shoes off first but do not bother to wash your feet because your dog will like the smell. When you jump up in pain/delight/ecstasy/agony/shock, check on the chart to see what is wrong with you. Pay your dog the going rate.

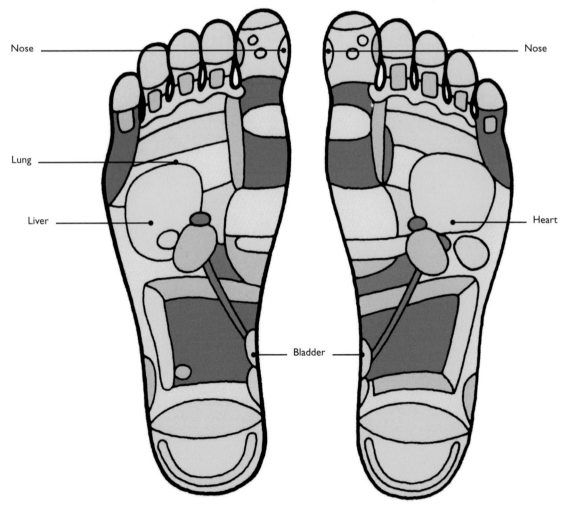

DAY 185

PRESS CONFERENCE

YOUR DOG IS A VERY IMPORTANT PERSON. How will the world know this unless you tell them? Call a press conference to spread the word. It's no longer necessary to wait for your dog to do anything tear-jerkingly brave/ useful/ intelligent/extraordinary/superlatively dumb to launch him publicly, as celebrity is now an end in itself, but it is very important that he looks good. Encourage him either to a) look surly and withdrawn and refuse to wag his tail b) yap constantly at a high pitch.

DAY 186

EXPLOIT YOUR DOG NO. 5

As a draft excluder

An ideal in-home activity for thick-haired breeds who are congenitally lazy; older, less frisky dogs make the best excluders.

zzzzz

DAY 187

DAY 188 Absurdity Training 2

Introduce some **random surreality** to your dog's life. Today teach him how to **play dead** every time he sees someone with a stick.

Every dog shall have its day

1 Choose a day of the week and rename it after your dog—for example, if he is called Fido, name it Fidoday.
2 Let your dog set the agenda for the day.
3 Do this for four weeks.
4 Test the strength of the cliché by taking notes to see if your dog's mood improves after having his day.

DAY 189

CANINE CLICHÉ TEST 1

SPOTDAY   BUTCHDAY   BENSONDAY   WEE-ANGUSDAY   TOWSERDAY   SPIKEDAY   TRIXIBELLEFIFI DAY

Make a plaster cast of your dog's paw/leg/tail/behind. Get your dog to sign it (if you haven't taught him to write yet, sign it for him). Then send it to MOMA to signify the power of the naïve gesture in a commodified art world ...

DAY 191

DOGGY PALMISTRY

Dip your **dog's paw** in mud, and press onto a piece of paper to make a print. Read your dog's palm.

🐾 FOOD LINE runs horizontally across paws.

🐾 LIFE LINE runs vertically across paws.

🐾 LOVE LINE runs diagonally across paws.

NUMEROLOGY DAY

Add together the numbers of your dog's birthdate (e.g. July 17 is 7+1+7=15). Then add the number of legs he has (e.g. 15+4=19). Reduce the final amount to a single digit. Look up what it means for your dog's present life and future. If you don't know your dog's birthdate—get your dog to choose his own number.

Find your dog's personal number

1 This is the number of the lead dog in any situation; or the dog who thinks he is the lead dog. Brave, smart, independent, first to learn new tricks, cleverest at stealing the turkey carcass after Thanksgiving. Also the dog most likely to turn rogue, bite small children, and pull rescue sled over crevasse.

2 Ideal number for a companion dog. Equable, co-operative, friendly—will put up with being dressed up by children, tolerate cats, and refrain from eating the hamster. Can become craven, a bit needy and co-dependent, and given to whining in corners when the master is away.

3 Bright, happy, optimistic dog, full of life, not afraid of self-expression. Always insanely keen to meet anybody, even burglars, and a very assiduous barker, even when there is nothing to bark about. Can be tiresomely boisterous and jump up at people who don't share his enthusiasm and joie de vivre.

4 Very well-behaved dog who likes to keep his basket neat. Very practical and able to carry several things in his mouth at the same time. Very efficient when it comes to bone burying. Likes walks at exactly the same time every day. Aversion to learning new tricks at any age and hates new bowls.

5 Big hearted, confident dog. Does not like to be led, and always looks for new walks when out. Loves dressing up and role-playing games, would be ideal film star or model material; always found with head in garbage looking for new experiences. Can be tetchy, snappy, and strains at the leash.

6 Loyal, devoted, responsible dog, suitable for a career as an assistant; can be relied upon to guard children, home, car. Domestic and home-loving, but can be stubborn, herd people into places they don't want to go, and won't let you out of your home when you are trying to go on vacation.

7 Excellent sniffer dog and hard worker; likes hide-and-seek games and purposeful walks with owner or on own. Can be friendly and charming, but has a strong relationship with his inner cat, so can be standoffish for no reason, and stay in basket when you want a cuddle; will only do tricks when offered a big reward.

8 Decisive executive dog, reliable and responsible, able to take charge of younger dogs; always decides own walk route; the dog most likely to alert people that the farm's on fire, or a small child has fallen down a well. Can be a bully, override owner's commands, and eat other members of the sled team.

9 Big, friendly slobbery kind of dog regardless of size. Always pleased to see everybody and ready to join in all games, do tricks, and share bones with lesser dogs. Can be very demanding of owner's time, and gets moody and restless. Forgets where bones are buried and then gets cross about it.

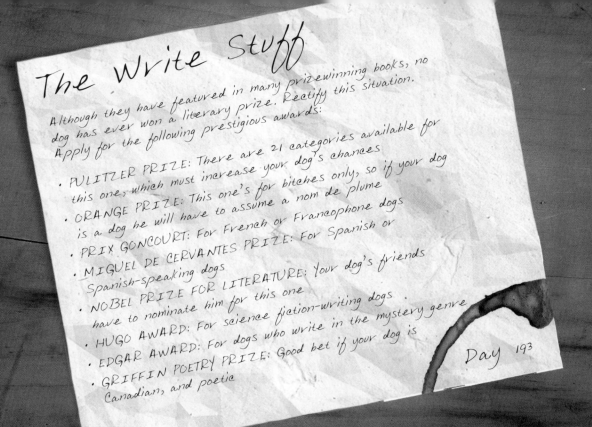

The Write Stuff

Although they have featured in many prizewinning books, no dog has ever won a literary prize. Rectify this situation. Apply for the following prestigious awards:

- PULITZER PRIZE: There are 21 categories available for this one, which must increase your dog's chances
- ORANGE PRIZE: This one's for bitches only, so if your dog is a dog he will have to assume a nom de plume
- PRIX GONCOURT: For French or Francophone dogs
- MIGUEL DE CERVANTES PRIZE: For Spanish or Spanish-speaking dogs
- NOBEL PRIZE FOR LITERATURE: Your dog's friends have to nominate him for this one
- HUGO AWARD: For science fiction-writing dogs
- EDGAR AWARD: For dogs who write in the mystery genre
- GRIFFIN POETRY PRIZE: Good bet if your dog is Canadian, and poetic

Day 193

DAY 194

LET SLEEPING DOGS LIE

CANINE CLICHÉ TEST 2

WHAT DID I MISS?

1. Wait for your dog to go to sleep.
2. Do not wake him; do not rattle food cans or offer walks.
3. See how long he lies there before waking up of his own accord.

DAY 195

NEVER AGAIN!

THE HAIR OF THE DOG

1. Get your dog drunk.
2. Note down what you have given him.
3. Next day give him some more.
4. Assess whether his hangover is cured.

DÉJÀ VU*UV ÁLÈD*

Day 196: Go back and repeat Day 25

It was such fun the first time around.

Vertical walking

Why should walks be horizontal? Spend the day going up in the elevators of tall buildings with your dog and then walking down.

Cuisine Chiennois

CRAFT your DOG'S DINNER into a designer-looking food dish, USING dog BISCUITS and TREATS as decoration.

I hope it's **meat!**

Contrasting colors tantalize the senses and produce a vivid synesthetic charge.

A delicate coulis of gravy and bonemeal serves ... hang on, dogs are color blind. Damn, three hours wasted.

The virgin purity of the dish emphasizes the richness of the tonal palette.

DAY 199

SAINT
DOG

Start a petition to HAVE YOUR DOG CANONIZED. He will need to have performed two miracles, although this is at the Pope's discretion.

POSSIBLE MIRACLES

Hair of the dog Apply hair to forehead after a night on the town and be revived.
Dogmata Display wounds of crucifixion on the paws.
Exorcism Chase a herd of pigs over the cliff.
Lazarus Bark very loud at night and wake the dead.

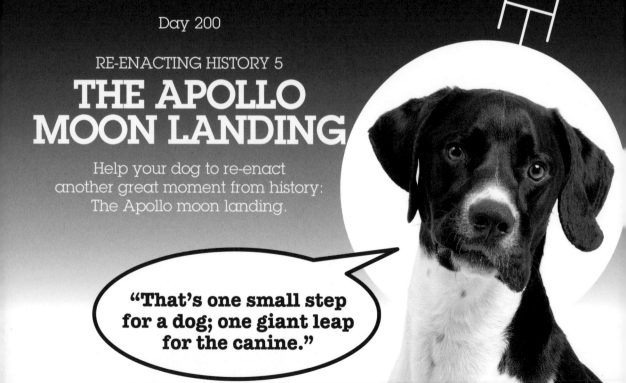

Day 200

RE-ENACTING HISTORY 5
THE APOLLO MOON LANDING

Help your dog to re-enact another great moment from history: The Apollo moon landing.

"That's one small step for a dog; one giant leap for the canine."

Dog Stars 2

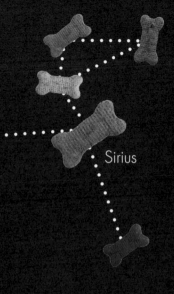

Sirius

In the second part of your dog's astronomy course, show him Canis Major (Big Dog); this is the home of the Dog Star Sirius, the brightest star in the sky (apart from the Sun). Don't let it go to his head. Canis Major is a northern constellation and it represents the hunting dog belonging to Orion. The alpha is Sirius.

DAY 201

CANIS MAJOR

DAY 202

YOU WILL FEEL VERY SLEEPY . . .

Have your dog hypnotized:

Find out who he was in a past life.

DAY 203

PUT A PHOTO OF YOUR DOG ON EVERY TREE

IN THE NEIGHBORHOOD with a sign saying "Have you seen this dog?" Take the dog for a walk and see how many people challenge you.

Total number
of challenges

HAVE YOU SEEN THIS DOG?

DAY 204

PUT A PHOTO OF YOUR DOG ON EVERY TREE

IN THE NEIGHBORHOOD
with a sign saying
"Have you seen this
dog?" Take the dog
for a walk DISGUISED
WITH DARK GLASSES
and see how many
people challenge
you this time.

total number
of challenges

Magnetize your dog's dog tags (weak force only) so that he sticks to metal objects. Film the hilarious results. stream live on the net.

*DAY 205

206

Stretch your Dog's Intellect

1: The Novel

Lock your dog in his kennel with food, water, and a keyboard and don't let him out until he has written the great American Novel.

Digger Dog
Trenching Terrier

Dogs like digging. You don't. Why not harness this excess excavatory energy? When tackling stubborn weeds, a good terrier can get right down to the roots. If your dog is bright, and has big paws, train him to double trench for asparagus or celery.

TIP: Use smaller breeds to make divot holes when sowing. Encourage them to run in parallel lines across freshly turned soil.

DAY 207

DAY 208

4 TODAY!

It is four years, in dog years, since you and your dog started on this project.

Celebrate together
Make a cake
Give a gift
Send a card
Prepare a special treat

HAPPY 4TH BIRTHDAY

profile   friends ▼   inbox ▼   home   logout

dogface

Name Here Please
What are you doing right now?

Relationship status   entry here pls
Birthday   entry here pls

Mini-Feed

DAY 209

Set up your dog's profile on Face Book. OK, so all dogs have one these days. Hack into the profile when he is offline and change his breed or photograph and his Scrabulous score details. That will teach him to have more friends than you.

Self-Assistance Dog

Co-author a self-help book for dogs with your dog. Do not rip this one off or we will sue. Think up snappy title (Who Buried My Bone?; Dogs Are From Sirius, Owners Are From Earth; Dogs Who Love Lamp Posts Too Much, etc.) Go on Oprah to promote your self-help book. Podcast from your back-yard. Agree to split royalties 30-30-40 (40% for us, because we thought of it). Get disgustingly rich. Buy your dog a mansion. Hire a team of ghost writers and their dogs to write the follow-up on pittance wages. Buy your dog a small country.

DAY 210

LOYALTY ROLE MODELS

Is your dog rolling around in ecstasy in front of complete strangers? When you come back from work is he not standing at the door looking keen? Does he stare soppily at your not-very-best-friend and spurn you when she offers a treat? To get him back in line, expose him to some hardcore loyalty examples. Reinforce the training with a treat if he sits still throughout the film, story, or song.

INSPIRING ICONS

Greyfriars Bobby
Old Shep
Old Yeller
Hachiko (*Japan's most faithful dog*)
Argus (*Odysseus's dog*)
Bullseye (*Bill Sykes's Dog*)

DAY 211

World of Color

Dogs see mostly in black and white, which is why they so often have a rigid outlook on things, and also why they prefer Laurel and Hardy to Cheech and Chong. You can address this by fitting your dog with colored contact lenses. This will cleanse his doors of perception and lead him to see things as they really are.

SHADOW ART

Turn out the main light, set up some light sources, and display shadow art with your dog. Teach him to make species appropriate moves such as for a rabbit or cat.
Remember a dog does not have opposable thumbs.

day
213

DAY 214

Do you really think your dog likes being called Sabre? Or Hannibal? Or Mr. Fluffy? Of course not. He has his own name for himself. An exclusive TBWCYDL* poll reveals the top ten canine names.

TOP TEN DOG NAMES

If dogs could name themselves...

WOOF

Most dogs call themselves Woof because that is easiest for them to say. It does not bother them that other dogs are also called Woof.

BIG

This popular name reflects how all dogs think of themselves, even if they are, in the scheme of things, very small dogs.

GRRR

No. 3 in the list, rather ominously, because this is what some dogs like to call themselves to emphasize their ferocity and aggressive tendencies.

WAG

A name that friendly, happy, cheerful dogs give themselves because it describes what they do with their tails all day.

MEAT

This name is an example of sympathetic magic; dogs who call themselves Meat are either badly treated or greedy (and are looking out for food).

HOT

Mostly used as a street name by younger, cockier dogs of all genders, advertising how they feel almost all of the time.

HISS

An onomato-poeaic name some dogs like because it describes so well the sound of their second favorite activity.

STICK

One of the three names to make it to the top ten in recognition of a dog's favorite activity; Stick is often used by playful dogs.

CHASE

Another activity name that is popular with athletic, energetic dogs; it is often hyphenated with Cats, Cars, or Balls.

DIRT

An old-fashioned name making a comeback among middle-class dogs in its meaning as "stuff you can dig up and bury bones in."

* The name of this book, you donut.

DAY 215

GIVE A DOG A BAD NAME

1. Choose a bad name for your dog (Hitler, Dahmer, Cheney).

2. Call him by that name; make him a dog tag with the name on it.

3. Monitor his behavior to see if he gets worse; if so, how much worse.

GRRRRRRRRR! GRRRR!

CANINE CLICHÉ TEST 3

POL POT

DAY 216

RANDOM FANS

Send signed photographs to everyone whose name begins with a "D."

Darling D
yours forever
xxxxxxxx

DAY 217

PUBLIC TRANSPOR CHALLENGI

LET YOUR DOG GET COMPLETE FILTHY, THEN TRY TO TAKE HIM ON PUBLIC TRANSPORTATION.

Test your powers of persuasion ("My dog just rescued two children from the river, which is why he smells like a stagnant pond") and your dog's appealingness.

INCREDIBLE JOURNEY

You know that movie where two dogs and a cat wander the wilds of Canada looking for their humans? Show it to your dog, then move to Canada and wait for him to find you. If you already live in Canada, skip this project and repeat day 109.

DAY 218

OUTSOURCE YOUR DOG'S JOBS: 6

WALKING

General all-rounder needed to drag handler out in all weathers twice a day.

SKILLS/QUALITIES REQUIRED

- Strong neck for leash-straining purposes.
- Superior slalom skills for inter-leg weaving
- Unerring sense of direction
- Robust foot pads

WOLF THERAPY

Is your dog losing his essential dogness? Is he denatured by 21st urban life? Why not treat him to an Iron Wolf Weekend where he can re-learn how to run in packs, howl across vast empty spaces, catch his own dinner, fight for his pack position, etc. Sessions held at our ranches in Montana, Wyoming, and New Jersey. www.runwithwolves.com

YAPPING TOO MUCH?

DAY 220

DOG WARRIORS

Form a gang with like-minded dogs. You do not have to be all the same breed. Dress in matching bandanas. Roam the subway looking mean until taken to the dog pound.

Apply to be First Dog

The White House* is always in need of a cute mutt to soften the presidential image. Apply for the post in the name of your dog.

* If you don't live in the US, apply to the relevant head of state. For example, UK dogs could apply for a post as HM Corgi.

DAY 222

LET YOUR DOG DO YOUR JOB

King Eystein ruled Norway between 1104 and 1123. His people, or folk, were so naughty that he decided to punish them by **letting the dog Suening rule in his place for three years**. Suening routinely **signed decrees with with paw-prints**, and Norway did not fall apart. Neither will your company. Announce that your dog is covering for you while you take a sabbatical.

N.B. This could backfire; when you return he may have a corner office and the ear (literally) of the CEO.

VERY IMPORTANT DOG

REPURPOSE YOUR DOG 2

Your dog spends a lot of time sitting on the rug in front of the TV. Why not repurpose him and expand his skill base by training him in remote retrieval?

One of modern life's most irritating minor frightfulnesses is losing the remote control for the TV/DVD/music system. Your dog can be both beautiful and useful, and prevent generational war in families, if he is trained to find it.

DAY 223

1. Let your dog sniff the remote control while you say the word "REMOTE."

2. Hide it down the back of the sofa/under the lounge chair/in the refrigerator*.

3. Command "FETCH + REMOTE."

4. Reward him when he finds it.

* Advanced work, so do the sofa/lounge chair task first.

Stretch your **Dog's Intellect**

2: GUT feeling

Lock your dog in the cellar with water, food, abacus, and a notepad. Don't let him out until he has formulated a GUT (Grand Unification Theory) of everything.

DAY 224

do nothing day

day 225

woof!
woof!

whimper.....whimper.....woof

Don't keep a dog and bark yourself?

1. Keep a dog. You are already doing this, so no instructions needed.

2. Gag him for 24 hours.

3. Whenever a barking opportunity comes up, do it yourself.

4. Note down the pros and cons of keeping a dog and barking yourself to test the truth of the cliché.

DAY 227

HOWLAOKE

RECORD YOUR DOG HOWLING TO A FAVORITE TUNE AND TAKE A SAMPLE. MAKE A HIP-HOP RECORD FOR A RINGTONE.

DAY 228

HOWLIN' HARMONY

Form a **close harmony singing group** with some like-minded dogs.

Plan a world tour to show off their talents to a wide, appreciative audience.

Bark Code No.3

(هو هو)

Your dog can now bark in Japanese and Chinese; if he is the kind of dog that enjoys a real challenge, try him on Arabic. Dogs don't have a great reputation in the Arabic world unless they are Salukis, the elegant and much prized dogs with the longest pedigree in the world (going back 7,000 years).

DAY 229

ARABIC

YOU CANNOT BE SIRIUS

READ your dog's HOROSCOPE in today's NEWSPAPER to him and see if it comes TRUE.

> You will meet a tall, dark stranger

Dog Stars No.3

Here is a star picture for the dumber dog. Canis Minor (the Lesser Dog) has got only two stars worth bothering about, so is easy to learn.

Procyon

Canis Minor is a northern constellation, representing, according to some astronomers, another of Orion's hounds. The alpha is Procyon.

CANIS MINOR

HOUNDINI

TIE YOUR DOG UP THOROUGHLY AND PUT HIM IN A BOX. MAKE SURE THERE IS ENOUGH AIR AND THAT HE HAS WATER. SEE HOW LONG HE TAKES TO GET OUT. MAKE HIM PRACTICE UNTIL HE IS REALLY GOOD. WHEN HE CAN DO IT IN UNDER 10 SECONDS, GET HIM AN AGENT AND A CONTRACT.

DAY 233

BATH FUN

NO DOGS LIKE BATHS, but maybe that's because baths are too dull. Spice up your dog's hygiene routine by introducing a PLAYFUL ELEMENT.

When out walking, THROW HIM unexpectedly into a water feature; pond in the park, municipal water fountain, or architectural intervention in a downtown atrium. DO THIS RANDOMLY and AT DIFFERENT times.

Different Smell

Change your dog's brand of shampoo and see if he becomes more attractive to the opposite sex.

Day 234

Some suggested substances/ materials:
* Wheatgerm
* Umbrella handles
* Dental floss
* Turnips
* Chocolate milk
* Paperclips

Absurdity Training 3: Pointless Sniffing

DAY 235

Train your dog to sniff out blameless substances, bark like mad when he finds them, and corner the carrier until the cops come. For added authenticity, get him a reflective jacket with "Homeland Security" printed on it.

STEPFORD *Dogs*

Show your love for your dog by dressing alike. Match T-shirts. Make yourself a collar and muzzle exactly like his. Rent yourself and your dog out for events.

Day 236

SOLIDARITY WITH THE ENEMY DAY

Chain you and your dog to the town hall railings to campaign for cat rights*.

DAY 237

*Cats have no legal rights. On the other hand, they have no legal responsibilities and cannot be held liable for anything, so they may not be too pleased if you win Congress over.

Dogs on Hogs

Ditch your car and buy a motorbike so your dog can experience the open road. He will need a tasseled jacket and a bandana. Look out for rednecks.

DAY 238

DAY 239

DOG RACER

Purchase a GERBIL to create a gaudily dressed "JOCKEY." Tape him to your dog's back, and RE-CREATE the exciting life of a thoroughbred RACE HORSE for your canine companion.

Offer him a treat if he can take a tumble in the sixth at the Kentucky Derby.

DAY 240

Paws for Thought

Play doggy charades with your dog as a prop. Act out as many dog expressions as you can from the following:

Let Sleeping Dogs Lie

It's a Dog's Life

His Bark Is Worse Than His Bite

You score points only if a neutral observer can guess correctly.

day
241

ECODOG 6

xxxxxxxxxxxxxxxxxxxxxxxxx

Knit your dog a sweater out of its own hair:

1) Shave dog
2) Collect hair
3) Spin into yarn
4) Knit sweater
5) Place on dog

DOG CHING

Let your dog make all your life decisions for the day. Find six flat sticks. Write an intention or activity on each one and throw them all at random; follow the instructions on whichever one he brings back. If you want another decision, collect the sticks and repeat the process.

DAY 242

Naturism Day

Get back to nature. Do your normal day, but naked:

🐾 Take all your clothes off.
🐾 Take your dog's collar off.
Be careful.

DAY 243

Spiritual Leanings 2:
Is he a Buddhist?

You have no idea of your dog's spiritual state. Maybe he is a Buddhist. To see if he is:

----

1) Dress him in yellow robes, or at least a yellow collar.
2) Change his daily ration to rice and lentils.
3) Plant a Bo tree for him to sit under.
4) Hang some bells from his kennel.
5) Draw mandalas for him.
6) Say "Om" whenever you want his attention.

Dog Games 1
Blind Dog's Buff

Teach your dog to play your games for a change. That will get him out of his ball/stick/squeaky toy mindset. Plus he will get invited to more interesting parties.

Tie a blindfold over your dog's eyes. Then spin him round and see how long he takes to catch you all.

DAY 246

KNOW YOUR PARASITES
ROUNDWORM

On Day 32, you taught your dog the lifecycle of the flea; follow up with the life cycle of the roundworm. That way he can't claim he wasn't told when it's worm pill time again.

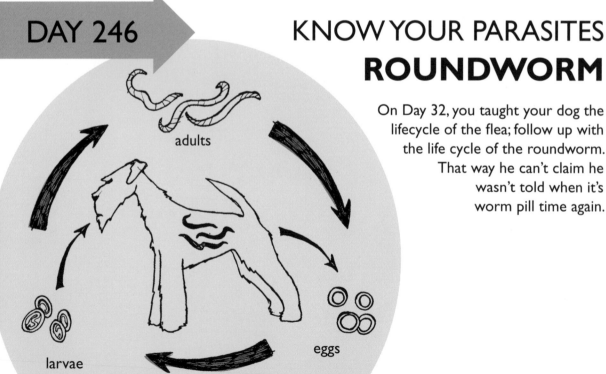

adults

larvae

eggs

Masterclass 6

HOW TO BURY A BONE

YOU WILL NEED

- Rubber gloves
- Small spade
- Bone

You teach your dog how to beg: let him teach you some of his skills. Today he will teach you HOW TO BURY A BONE.

You try: Get down on all fours in front of the selected burial spot. Use small trowels and scrape the soil vigorously backward, away from you. Do not fling it too far because you need to put it all back in again. When you get proficient with the trowels, try it using just your hands.

BONE BURIAL

Mounds of earth

Backyard (unspoiled)

Cute dog

Ground

Dog (still cute)

Juicy bone

Deep hole

1. Let your dog show you the best place to dig in the backyard or local park. It should be secluded and the soil easy to dig yet robust enough to hide whatever you're burying. A nice loamy mix is best.

2. Your hole needs to be at least three times as deep as the object you are burying. Do not worry if you go too deep, although this may make retrieval of the object difficult.

Backyard (will need tidying)

Cute dog with juicy bone

Hole (still deep)

Backyard (making good)

Cute dog (with dirty paws)

Filled hole

3. Dig the hole so that it has slanting sides and a flattish bottom. Place the bone, or a treasure of your choice, at the bottom. Hold it in your mouth and just drop it in.

4. Turn around (on all fours) with your back to the hole, and scrape all the earth you dug up back in. Pace around the filled hole several times, maybe dragging some plant matter over it.

TIP Spray some of your signature scent/aftershave on the spot so that you can find it by smell when you return to it.

DAY 248

TALK TO YOUR DOG
IN HIS OWN LANGUAGE

1 Basic Barking

Before you go on to more sophisticated communication, you must master basic barking. Fortunately it is not difficult. You simply put your lips together and say "oof," twice. When you have perfected this, experiment by varying the pitch and volume.

DAY 249

Test the system

Perform a public service by attempting to smuggle your dog through check-in in your hand luggage to test airport security.

THE 365 NAMES OF DOGS

Abby Achilles **ALGY** PUG *Alice* **Alistair** Amber **ANGUS** *Apollo* Archie Argos **ASH** **ASTRO** *Bandit* **Barney** Basket **BAXTER** *Baz* Beano Beauregard **BEAUTY** **BEETHOVEN** *Belle* **Ben** Benjy **BIFF** *Bilbo* Bingo Biscuit **BLACKIE** **BLAZE** *Boatswain* **Bobby** Bolivar **BONNIE** Bonzo Boogie Boots **BORIS** **BOUNCER** *Bracken* **Brandy** Bravo **BRIAN** *Griffin* Bron Bruce **BRUISER** **BRUNO** *Brutus* **Buck** **BUDDY** **BUFFY** Bullseye Buster Butch *Buttons* **Cadpig** Cagney **CANDY** *Caper* Caprice Casey **CASPAR** **CENTAUR** *Cerberus* **Charlie** Chelsea Cherry **CHESTER** Chief **CHILI** **CHIP** *Chuck* **Clarissa** Clifford **CLYDE** *Coco* Cody **COOKIE** Cooper Cossack **DAISY** *Darby* Davey *Diefenbaker* Digby **DINAH** **DINGO** *Diva* **DIXIE** **Doc** *Dogmatix* *Domino* Don *Doodles* **DOPEY** **DOUGAL** *Duchess* Duff *Duke* **DUSTY** *Dylan* **Earl** Eddie *Edison* Elektra *Ella* **ELVIS** Ernie *Fancy* **Fang** Fats **FIDO** *Fifi* Fizz **FLASH** *Fluffy* Fluke Flush *Fly* **FRASIER** **FRED** Freeway *Frieda* Frostie Gelert **GENERAL** Geordie George *Geronimo* **GIN** Ginger *Gnasher* **GOLIATH** **GOOBER** **GRINGO** Grip *Gromit* Grundy **GUNNER** **Gus** *Gussie* **GYPSY** *Hamish* **Happy** *Harry* **HARVEY** Hector **HENRY** *Herbie* **Hip-Hop** Hitch Hobnob **HOBO** **HOLLY** Homer **Hong Kong** **Phooey** Hooch *Horatio* **HUCKLEBERRY HOUND** *Humphrey* **IGGY** *Inca* **IZZIE** *Jack* Jake **JASPER** **JENNY** *Jess* **Jingo** **JIP** *Jock* *Joey* John **JOINER** K-9 *Kaiser* **KEEPER** *Kep* *Kerouac* Kerry *Kim* *Kipper* *Kojak* *Krypto* **LADY** **LAFAYETTE** *Laika* Lassie **LAYLA** **LEON** *Lizzie* **LOLA** **LOTTIE** *Luath* **Lucky** **LUCY** *Lulu* Lupus *Mabel* **MAC** Maggie **MAGIC** *Major* *Marbles* **MARTHA** Max **MEG** **MERRY** **MILO** *Mitzi* **MOJO** **MOLLY** **MONTMORENCY** **MORGAN** **Moss** *Muffin* **Mungo** *Murray* **MUTTLEY** **MYCROFT** *Nana* Napoleon **NELSON** **Nero** *Nipper* **OLD YELLER** Ollie **ORSON** *Oscar* Paddy Patch **Peaches** **PEG** Penfold *Percy* Perdita Pete **PETRA** *Pharoah* **Philip** Pickles **PILGRIM** *Pilot* **PIP** Pippin *Pirate* **PLUTO** *Pointy* **PONCHO** **PING** *Pongo* Pop **Poppy** **PORTHOS** Preston **Prince** **PUGNAX** *Rags* Ralf *Rascal* **REBEL** *Red* Rex Riley **RIN TIN TIN** Rip **ROCKY** **Roger** *Rowlf* Roly *Roobarb* **ROSCOE** **ROSIE** *Rover* **Rowdy** *Rowsby* **RUFFLES** Rufus Rusty **SABLE** **SADIE** Saffron **Sally** Sam *Samson* **SANDY** Santa's Little Helper *Sasha* **SCAMP** Scamper *Scooby Doo* Scooter **Scottie** **SCRUFFY** Seymour Shadow **SHADRACH** *Sheba* Shelby **Sherry** *Skip* **SLINKY** *Smiffy* **SMOKIE** *Smudge* *Sniff* **Snook** *Snoopy* *Snowy* **SOX** *Sparky* **SPIKE** Spot **STANLEY** *Stingo* **Streaker** Stumpy *Suki* **SULTAN** Suzy **TAFF** *Tallulah* **Tammy** *Tango* **TED** *Texas* Thimble **Thor** *Thorn* **TIGER** *Timmy* **Tinker** *Tinkerbell* **TINY** *Tip* Titan *Titus* Toby **TOFFEE** *Tommy* **TONTO** Topaz **Topsy** *Toto* *Tramp* **TRAVIS** Trey **TRICKIE-WOO** *Trixie* Trojan Truman **Trusty** *Turbo* **TYKE** **VESTA** Vincent **WELLARD** *Wellington* Whisky **Wolf** *Yofi* **YOSHA** **ZACK** Zorro

* DAY 251 *
Stand Up Straight

Develop a stand-up comedy routine, observing life's little vicissitudes in a surrealistic manner, employing an elegant vocabulary deployed in a down home accent, a sprinkling of knowing cultural references, a catch phrase, and some rude words. Feature your dog as the straight man. Take it on the road to all the major comedy festivals.

REPURPOSE YOUR DOG 3

Increase your dog's self-esteem by encouraging him to earn his own income and pay for his keep. Assuming he is not a professional—sled puller, seeing eye dog, hearing dog, racing dog, police dog, rescue dog, guard dog, film star—stick with domestic tasks he can perform with pride and that will be useful to you.

Try this simple one if your dog failed on the remote retriever job, (Day 223), to rebuild his confidence. Train him to bark four times when your eggs have been boiling for four minutes.

1. Command him to SIT while you put water in the pan and onto the stove.
2. Command STAY when water reaches boiling point and you put the eggs in.
3. Command BARK when four minutes (or your optimum egg boiling time) is up.

DAY 252

253

BIG BANG

BUILD YOUR DOG HIS OWN NUCLEAR FALLOUT SHELTER. TRAIN HIM TO ENTE IT WHEN HE HEARS THE COMMAND "WMC (WEAPONS OF MASS DESTRUCTION).

DESERT DOG

Shock your dog out of complacency again. Transform the yard overnight by dumping builder's sand and a palm tree in a pot. If it is gloomy weather, add patio heaters or super-trouper stage lights. Put your dog's kennel in the cellar and replace it with a Bedouin tent. When he wakes up in the morning he will think he is in the Sahara. That will be a nice change for him, non?

DAY 254

DAY 255

Old Slipper Guide

A catalog of tried and tested Old Slippers for your dog
to look at in the long winter evenings.

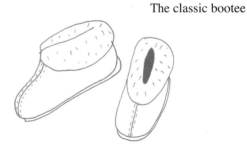

The classic bootee

Husky delight

Something delicate

Only for the hardcore

day 256

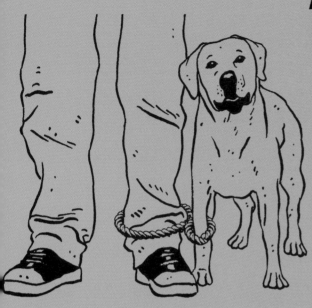

ARE FIVE LEGS BETTER THAN SIX?

Find out by going five-legged for the day. Tie one of your dog's legs to one of yours. If you have a big dog this could be tricky. If you have a small dog it could be tricky as well. In fact, we think we know the answer to this question already, but we thought it would be amusing to let you figure it out.

Extreme Sports 3: Zero Gravity

DAY 257

Treat your dog to some zero gravity. Humans have to pay a fortune to go up in a space shuttle just to float like a butterfly, but you can do the same for your dog with a few balloons—just enough to lift him off the ground. This probably won't work for a St. Bernard.

Good Dog Day

Share a diet of brown rice and alfalfa shoots with your dog for a week. Send the money you save to Oxfam, or to a dogs' charity of your choice.

Day 258

MAKE YOUR DOG A PIÑATA DAY

Treat your dog to a random fiesta. Make a large cat-shaped piñata out of colored paper and fill it with delicious treats: chews, choc drops, crackers, balls, rubber toys, sausages. Hang it from the branch of a tree, or from a light fitting if you have an indoor dog. Throw sticks at it* until it breaks open and all the treats cascade onto your dog. Mexican breeds will find this particularly barkworthy.

*For extra fun, your dog can retrieve the ones that miss.

DAY 259

DAY 260

5 TODAY!

It is five years, in dog years, since you and your dog started on this project.

Celebrate together
Make a cake
Give a gift
Send a card
Prepare a special treat
Organize an outing

HAPPY 5TH BIRTHDAY

DOG GAMES 2: Musical Baskets

DAY 261

Another human game for your dog. Invite some of his friends around and supply one fewer basket than there are dogs. Arrange baskets in a circle and encourage the dogs to run around them, leading the way yourself*. Have a fellow owner play rousing music that all the dogs like. When the music stops, shout the command "BASKET!" All dogs should hurl themselves at the baskets, but there won't be enough. Last dog standing is out and has to sit for the rest of the game. Remove a basket and continue until one dog triumphs.

* Do not attempt to get in a basket

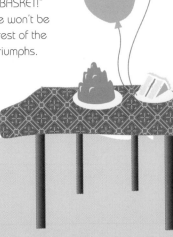

DAY 262

Sloooo**o**o...o...o...o...oow Moooooo...oooo...ooo

Today do everything you always do but at half the speed so that you appear to be in slow motion. This will mean shouting commands and orders in a very low voice and stretching out the sound. See how long it takes for your dog to adjust to your new pace.

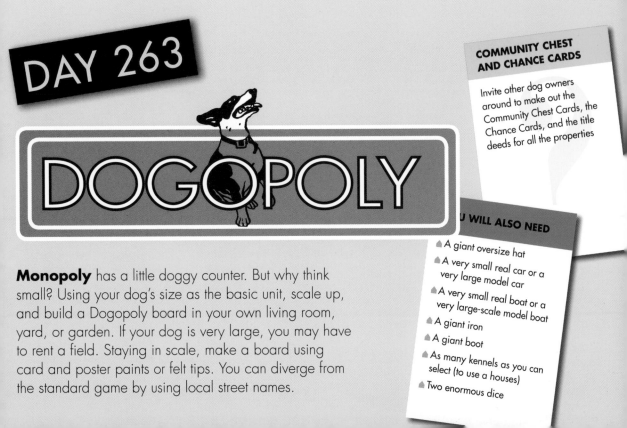

DAY 263

DOGOPOLY

Monopoly has a little doggy counter. But why think small? Using your dog's size as the basic unit, scale up, and build a Dogopoly board in your own living room, yard, or garden. If your dog is very large, you may have to rent a field. Staying in scale, make a board using card and poster paints or felt tips. You can diverge from the standard game by using local street names.

COMMUNITY CHEST AND CHANCE CARDS

Invite other dog owners around to make out the Community Chest Cards, the Chance Cards, and the title deeds for all the properties

YOU WILL ALSO NEED

- 🐾 A giant oversize hat
- 🐾 A very small real car or a very large model car
- 🐾 A very small real boat or a very large-scale model boat
- 🐾 A giant iron
- 🐾 A giant boot
- 🐾 As many kennels as you can select (to use a houses)
- 🐾 Two enormous dice

Hat Day

Give your dog, and yourself, a rest from all this life-changing by letting him doze in his basket while you spend the day making him a nice hat. Try a Stetson or a Borsalino if he is a fierce breed, or a vintage butcher's straw boater with sausage link trim for the more traditional dog.

DAY 264

DAY 265

LIKED IT TOO!

IT'S A DOG EAT DOG WORLD

❶ Give your dog cooked dog for dinner.

❷ Note down his reactions.

❸ Access the truth of the cliché.

CANINE CLICHÉ TEST 5

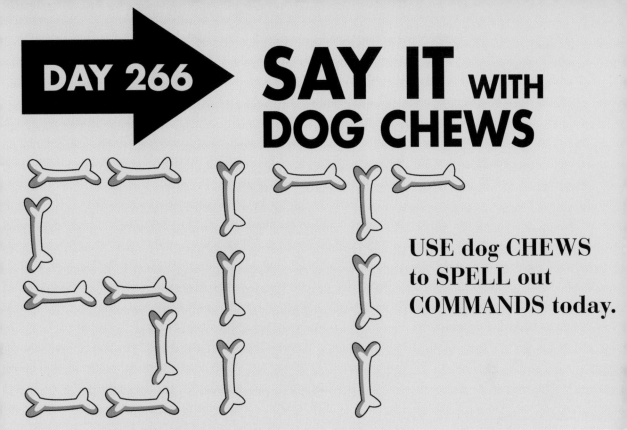

DAY 266 → SAY IT WITH DOG CHEWS

USE dog CHEWS to SPELL out COMMANDS today.

REPURPOSE YOUR DOG 4

On day 252 you trained your dog to be an eggtimer. Today you will teach him to truffle for keys.

1. Hold relevant keys under your armpit for a bit so that they are properly imbued with your scent.

2. Show them to your dog and say "KEYS."

3. Throw the keys into a random corner.

4. Give a command "FETCH + KEYS."

5. Give a reward.

After a few practice runs, your dog should be able to find your lost keys in under two minutes—ideal when you are late for work/plane/school/baby delivery. This will miraculously lower your stress levels and do wonders for your human relationship, if you have one.

DAY 267

BE A VET FOR A DAY

Put the boot on the other paw by allowing your dog to play Vets and Veterinary Nurses with a friend. Provide scrubs, hypodermics, rectal thermometers, and cuddly toys for patients.

DAY 268

A Dog's GUIDE TO TREES

Best tree to cock your leg against (or not)

Aaaahhh!

GOOD TREES as selected by our panel	
OAK	Good solid trunk, plenty of shade in summer, falling acorns could harm smaller breeds.
ASH	Very hard wood, smooth, slick surface for ease of flow.
ELM	The interlocking grain means no splitting, so a splinter-free experience; once ubiquitous, now quite rare.
BEECH	Lots of ridges at the bottom so excellent for the shorter dog; also has pleasant malty smell.
DOG WOOD	Compact size, with a trunk diameter of 12 inches (30 cm), so not for the larger dog.
SYCAMORE	Scaly bark on mature trees offers additional back scratching opportunities.

Aarrgghh!

BAD TREES for use only in an emergency	
HOLLY	To be avoided for obvious reasons; and the berries give you diarrhea.
SPRUCE	The trunk is knobbly and unreachable and you will never get the needles out of your coat.
YEW	Scaly brown bark that comes off in flakes; and it's poisonous.
WILLOW	Unreliable; believed to uproot itself and wander about in the dead of night looking for victims.
RUBBER	Leaks latex and could result in unpleasantly sticky situation.
BLACK LOCUST	Furrowed, poisonous bark; beware, lots of these in parks and public places.

Musical Ears

Teach your dog to waggle his ears in time to the Star Spangled Banner/Advance Australia Fair/God Save the Queen/La Marseillaise/ and hire him out for especially patriotic occasions. Don't count on making much money if you have a West Highland Terrier.

CROON ALONG

Sing with your dog all day today, as you do everyday tasks. Choose a beat and get into a rhythm. Here are two to get you started.

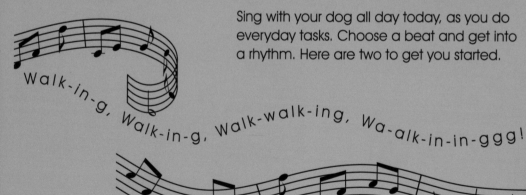

Walk-in-g, Walk-in-g, Walk-walk-ing, Wa-alk-in-in-ggg!

Sit, sit, sit, sit, sit-sit, sit, sit-sit, sit-sit, s-i-i-t

DAY 272

LEARN TO TANGO WITH YOUR DOG

start

The Tango was born in the working-class bars of Buenos Aires, Argentina. It is meant to be danced with your sister- or brother-in-law, wife's or husband's best friend, or any other off-limits person to whom you are perversely attracted.

DAY 273

DOG MUSIC

SAMEY DOGHOUSE
DRAW A STAVE. LET YOUR DOG WANDER OVER IT, PLAYING A TUNE.
GET A RECORDING CONTRACT, BECOME FAMOUS, AND GET RICH. SPORT A WACKY HAIRDO, GET TATTOOED, MARRY A LOSER, AND DON'T GO INTO REHAB. BE AN INSPIRATION FOR MILLIONS OF YOUNG PUPS AROUND THE WORLD.

Dog Stars 4

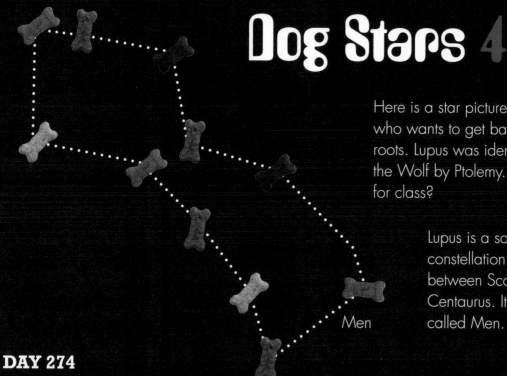

Here is a star picture for the dog who wants to get back to his roots. Lupus was identified as the Wolf by Ptolemy. How's that for class?

Lupus is a southern constellation that lies between Scorpius and Centaurus. Its alpha is called Men.

Men

DAY 274

LUPUS

DAY 275

Vice Versa

Surprise your dog tonight. Cook yourself a slap-up meal with steak and all the fixings, then when it is all ready, give it to your dog to eat while you chow down on the kibble★.

★Can encourage weight loss

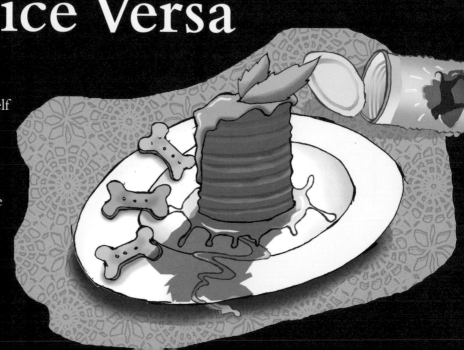

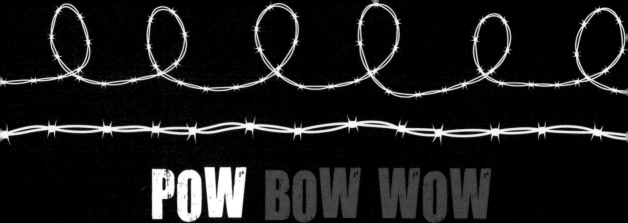

POW BOW WOW

Build your dog his own prison camp in the yard. He will need a hut to sleep in, a perimeter fence with barbed wire, and towers with high-power lamps. Leave him with a vaulting horse, enough balsa wood and canvas to build an escape glider, and pieces of wood to make tunnel props.

Get other owners in, and invite their dogs, to see if they will co-operate and which one of them will go maverick and ride away on a motorbike. Mount a 24-hour guard, using pump-action water pistols as your weapon of choice should any try to make a break.

A growl for help

Cover your dog's mouth in soap bubbles, and laugh contemptuously at those who shy away from your new "rabid" dog. Earn the respect of your neighbors by gently but deliberately prodding him and shouting "C'mon you great wet lettuce! Bite me!"

DAY 278

The Rules
- Round up the local dogs.
- **First to get laid wins.**

DOG SPEED DATING COMPETITION

Keeping a success score is just being cocky

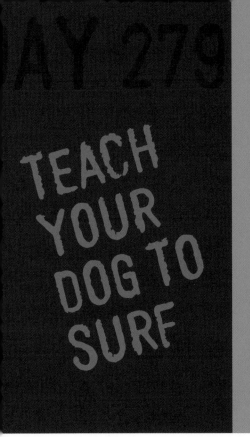

TEACH YOUR DOG TO SURF

SURF'S UP

Bark Code No.4

ГАВ ГАВ

If you want to move up some, and make friends with some Russian oligarchs, teach your dog to bark in Russian; then he can hang around uptown with borzois, tazis, Samoyeds, Siberian huskies and so on. Note that small Ukrainian dogs say "dzyau dzyau." It could make all the difference between shares in an oil pipeline or a one-way trip to the gulag.

DAY 280   **RUSSIAN**

Mingle with the Mighty

Find out which celebrities have dogs. Write to their dogs on their behalf and set up a playdate. If you succeed, sell your story to Gawker or Hello. Be aware that celebrity may rub off on your dog, and he might start demanding his own limo, stylist, and hand-shredded kobe beef on the hour.

Ann Owner

Bonzo Ciccone
Chateau Fabulous
Megarich Drive
Malibu
California 90263

DAY 281

DAY 282

BE BELGIAN FOR A DAY

Belgium gets a bad press. There is that joke about a famous Belgian. But Belgium has beautiful cities, wonderful beer, fabulous chocolate, and moules-et-frites. They even have a Peeing Boy as their national mascot. What's not to like? Your dog is, of course, on the side of the underdog, so spend a day in solidarity. All the better if you can do this on July 21, which is Belgium's National Day.

Famous Belgians

Rene Magritte	Jacques Brel	Antony van Dyck
Peter Paul Rubens	Toots Thielemans	Audrey Hepburn
James Ensor	Cesar Franck	Henri van der Velde
Leo Baekeland	Eddie Merckx	Dries van Noten
Hercule Poirot	Kim Clijsters	Ann de Meulenmeester
Adolphe Sax	Georges Simenon	Tintin
Django Reinhardt	Hieronymus Bosch	Plastic Bertrand

CITIZEN
DOG 3

TAKE YOUR DOG TO SEE HIS
POLITICAL REPRESENTATIVE.

Present his case for a
CANINE REFORM BILL.

REPURPOSE YOUR DOG 5

**Elsewhere you have repurposed your dog as a reflexologist, eggtimer, and a key truffler.
Today he can add to his career portfolio by training as a sock hound.**

1. Put the relevant socks on your feet for a bit so that they are properly imbued with your scent.

2. Show your dog the items and say "SOCKS."

3. Throw the socks into a random corner.

4. Give him a command "FETCH + SOCKS."

5. Give him a reward.

This is a very useful and cost-effective use of your dog. Everybody
always loses one of a pair of socks. If your dog can be trained to
find the missing one, you will save yourself a fortune on foot-based
accessories. Of course there is always the danger that your dog
will be abducted by aliens from the Planet of Lost Socks, but that's a risk
worth taking, especially since it won't be you suffering the bright lights and anal probe.

SPOT
THE
DOG

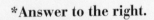

GO!

**HOW MANY DIFFERENCES CAN YOU FIND
BETWEEN THE TWO DOGS?**

*There are 25 differences between the two dogs.

*****Answer to the right.**

DAY 286

FAST
TRACK

*Teach your dog NOT TO
GET TOO COCKY. Enter him
at the local track and BET
ON HIM TO LOSE.*

TALK TO YOUR DOG
IN HIS OWN LANGUAGE

2. Walks

Walks in Dog is a simple, two-part vocalization (woof woof) with a short, high-pitched whine in between the two woofs. It may take you some time to get the pitch exactly right, but don't be afraid of repeating yourself until understood.

DAY 288

HOME FROM HOME

PLAN YOUR VACATION with your dog going only TO DOG-RELATED PLACES.

*From Latin canis, dog

PLACES TO GO

Barkley Sound, Canada

Dalmatia

Afghanistan

West Highlands

*Canary Islands

Berkshire

Isle of Dogs, London, England

Labrador

Dogger Bank

Pomerania

Airedale

Appenzell

Staffordshire

Newfoundland

Dog, Canada

Berkeley, California

Hounde, Upper Volta

Rottwell

Alaska

Yorkshire

Chihuahua

Alsace

SPIRITUAL LEANINGS 3: AMISH

You don't know which spiritual path your dog is following. Maybe he is Amish?
Try the following to see if he responds:

- Grow a beard.
- Feed him from hand-turned wooden bowls.
- Sell your car and buy a pony and trap.
- Speak to him only in German.
- Get rid of any diamante collars (yours as well).
- Invite his friends round for a kennel raising.

DAY 290 HOMING DOG

TEACH YOUR DOG HOW TO FIND HIS WAY HOME

➤ Start with small distances, then increase them until he can find his way home no matter how far away he is.

➤ A bribe of his favorite food will help here.

➤ When he is really good at getting home, no matter where you leave him, take him away and sell him. Pocket the cash.

➤ When he eventually escapes and finds his way home, do it again.

GROUND-DOG DAY

If your dog is being crotchety and unsociable, give him the following treatment.

1) Wake up him up every day at the same time, with the same music (e.g. *Do it Again* by Steely Dan).

2) Wear the same clothes every day and say the same things (you will need a script for this).

3) Give him exactly the same food in exactly the same bowl.

4) Go on exactly the same walk every day, stop in the same places; arrange to meet a friend in exactly the same spots.

DAY 291

WARNING: He may like this.

DOG TATS

DAY 292

TATTOOS YOUR DOG MAY ENJOY

SAUSAGES   BONES   RABBIT

DAY 293

TALK TO YOUR DOG
IN HIS OWN LANGUAGE

3: Transactional Yawning

This is the most difficult for you to master technically, because yawning is not transactional in humans. Open your mouth wide, then leave it open at the end of the yawn, obtrude the tongue and pant gently for a while. Use this when you want to calm your dog. Be careful not to fall asleep.

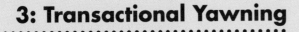

DAY 294
FINDING DOG

DOG IS GOD BACKWARDS.

FOUND A RELIGION in your dog's name.

Have a slogan ("In Dog We Trust") and **some commandments:** Sit, Stay, Heel, and so on.

DAY 295
REVEREND DOG

GET YOUR DOG ORDAINED ONLINE. Now he can wear a dog collar.

DAY 296

DOGS IN THE ARTS

Is your DOG an OIL PAINTING? Plenty have been. Get the BRUSHES OUT and try your hand. Here are some to look at.

EDWIN LANDSEER *Her Majesty's Favorite Pets* (1837). Queen Victoria's pooches (and a parrot).

EMANUEL DE WITTE *Interior of the Old Church in Delft* (1650–52). This features a dog with anti-clerical tendencies.

PIERRE BONNARD *Le Café* (1915). One of many with Mme. Bonnard and her dachshund.

ANDY WARHOL *Portrait of Maurice* (1976). What is it about dachshunds?

PHILIP REINAGLE *Portrait of an Extraordinary Musical Dog* (1805). King Charles spaniel with a taste for the virginals.

CASSIUS MARCELLUS COOLIDGE *Only a Pair of Deuces* (1903). Fat dogs playing poker.

FRANCISCO DE GOYA *The Dog* (1820). Not that there is much dog in it.

TITIAN *Venus of Urbino* (1538)—there's a dog who knows when he's well off.

JACK BUTLER YEATS *Jelly Jelly Jelly All Jelly* (c. 1900), a day at the whippet races.

DAY 297

LEARN TO WALTZ WITH YOUR DOG

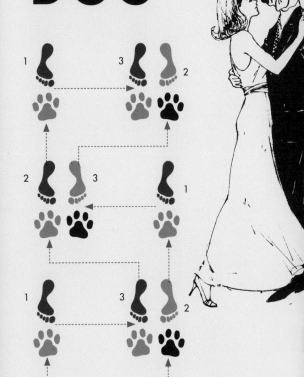

A development of Austrian peasant dances, the waltz was considered indecent when the Prince Regent introduced it to England in 1816, and indecorous when it was danced in Mrs Otis's Boston mansion in 1834. This was because partners held each other close; unsurprisingly it became very popular.

HOUNDTOOTH™

Leave your cell phone on the floor
and let your dog walk over it.
Talk to whoever your dog calls
when he steps on it.

DAY 299

TALK TO YOUR DOG
IN HIS OWN LANGUAGE

4 Heel

This is advanced stuff and should not be attempted
by the unlimber. Get down on all fours as near to
your dog's back leg as possible (right or left).
Shuffle after him when he walks, staying as
close as possible. Pant keenly as you go.

DAY 300

BE A CAT FOR A DAY

Bust your dog out of his comfort zone by treating him like a cat for a day. Punish any keen behavior and panting and encourage staring into corners. Replace his basket with a cat cushion, exchange a ball for a mouse, play a CD of birdsong, swap his dog tags for a bell, borrow a goldfish in a bowl. Purr at him.

Feline helpful tips for your dog

- Do not prick up your ears every time your owner speaks. Make him/her sweat.

- Do not rush when summoned. Get up slowly, stretch, sit down, have a wash, fall asleep.

- Do NOT, under any circumstances, fetch ANYTHING.

- It is your right to be on any bed, the comfiest chair, or anywhere else you fancy.

- Stand by the door and howl to be let out. Go out. Stand by the door and howl to be let in.

- Do not just wolf everything down. Practice turning your nose up in disdain at what is in the food bowl (this will be very hard, but work at it).

ears

The right sort of ears will help your dog get in character. We have provided a handsome set of cut-out ears for temporary use (right) but if your dog takes to walking on the feline side, make up a more robust set using a child's headband, some felt, fur fabric, and wire for stiffening. Make some for yourself as well. Wear them.

Notes:
_____
_____
_____
_____
_____
_____
_____
_____
_____
_____
_____
_____

cut here

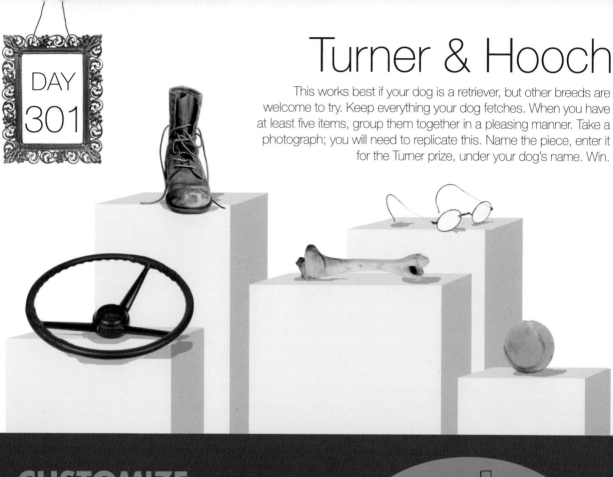

Turner & Hooch

This works best if your dog is a retriever, but other breeds are welcome to try. Keep everything your dog fetches. When you have at least five items, group them together in a pleasing manner. Take a photograph; you will need to replicate this. Name the piece, enter it for the Turner prize, under your dog's name. Win.

CUSTOMIZE YOUR KENNEL

Make up a mood board of interiors, fabrics, colorways etc. for your dog and let him sniff out which one suits his style. Help him realize his dream home, even if you think it sucks.

DAY 302

I'VE ALWAYS HANKERED AFTER A BIT OF MARTHA

A DOG'S HOME IS HIS CASTLE

NEW HOME, NEW HOME, SO GOOD I'VE NAMED IT TWICE

DAY 3O3
DOGUE

Let your dog CHOOSE YOUR WARDROBE for the day.

Let him sniff around in your closets and drawers, and pull out garments. Wear only what he gives you. If you get compliments, hire him out as a stylist.

SCRATCH AND SNIFF

ANISE

BLOOD

BONE

TREE BARK

DOG OF OPPOSITE SEX

DEAD SQUIRREL

FILLET STEAK

VOMIT

This page is impregnated with EIGHT DIFFERENT SCENTS that your DOG WILL SALIVATE OVER. You can't smell them, but you can FIND OUT WHICH ONES HE LIKES BEST.

Prêt à Marcher

Provide your dog with fashionable leash options so that he can suit his style to his mood for the day.

black tie

urban grunge

Boho

power chic

goth

DAY 306

DOGGY CASINO

Set up a casino for your dog; use a large-scale roulette wheel with his favorite ball on the roulette; play craps with giant furry dice; wear eye shades.

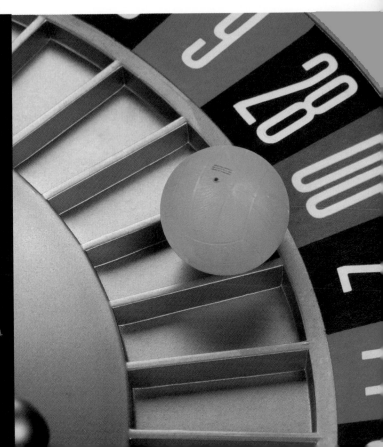

DAY 307

MAKE YOUR DOG FEEL INFERIOR 3

Is your dog getting a bit above himself?

Show him some dogs at the top of their game to prove he is not all that clever.

DAY 308

TALK TO YOUR DOG
IN HIS OWN LANGUAGE

5 Fetch

You may find it hard not to use your opposable thumbs here but it is essential to pick up the leash or stick in your mouth and carry it to your dog, where you should drop it at his paws.

FIRE HYDRANTS OF THE WORLD

Hong Kong

Cook Islands

Estonia

Italy

UK

Germany

France

Bahrain

Finland

Guinea Bissau

Canada

Yemen

Jordan

Senegal

Switzerland

USA

Costa Rica

DAY 309

Kyrgyzstan

Dog Dating

A day to embrace the strangeness of love. Suggest to your dog that he ventures away from his usual choice of bedfellow and tries something a little more recherché.

DAY 310

DAY 311   FAN CLUB DAY

Increase your dog's popularity by setting up a fan club.

★ Create a website and set up an email address for both canine and human fans to use.

★ Take a photo, get it signed (paw print), and add it to the website.

★ Run competitions for signed photos.

StarDogFanClub.com

http://stardogfanclub.com

STAR FAN **CLUB** Dog

- 🐾 Star Dogiography
- 🐾 Star Fashion Tips
- 🐾 Star Appearances
- 🐾 Star Blog
- 🐾 Star Photos

🐾 Enter here to win a signed photo

DAY 312

6 TODAY!

It is six years, in dog years, since you and your dog started on this project.

**Celebrate together
Make a cake
Give a gift
Send a card
Prepare a special treat
Organize an outing
Invite friends around**

HAPPY 6TH BIRTHDAY

Do something with this book

Put a copy of this book in your dog's basket. See what he does with it. Fill in the form on this page, and send it to us. We will prepare a statistical analysis.

DAY 313

WEE ON IT	
GROWL AT IT	
SLEEP ON IT	
IGNORE IT	
BURY IT	
CARRY IT AROUND IN HIS MOUTH ALL DAY	
READ IT	

DAY 314

TIME CAPSULE

Make a TIME CAPSULE and BURY IT

Make a time capsule out of one of your socks. Inside the capsule put a sample of what your dog is doing, eating, or playing with right now. Bury it and let him find it. Alright, it is a time capsule of half an hour ago, but that's a long time in dog years!

YAY!
GOODIES!

DAY 315

LEARN TO FOXTROT WITH YOUR DOG

QUICK

QUICK

SLOW

SLOW

QUICK

QUICK

SLOW

SLOW

start

Foxtrot
The Foxtrot was invented by Harry Fox, the American vaudeville artist. It was first seen in New York in 1914 and quickly became the most popular dance style of the twentieth century.

BONE ORIGAMI

Your dog has never experienced the lost art of bone origami. Today is the first day of the rest of his origami existence. Make the following shapes . . . cat, fire hydrant, truck.

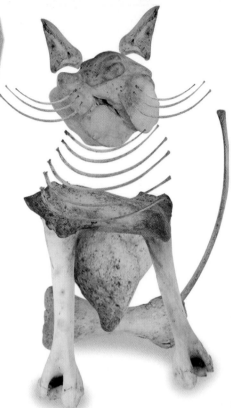

DAY 316

DAY 317
E-DOG

🐾 **Sign your dog up to Skype or MSN.**

🐾 **Meet other dogs online and let them bark at each other.**

🐾 **Obviously, don't give out your dog's real name.**

YOL = Yelp Out Loud • BS = Butt Sniff • ABS = Another Butt
Sniff • LFY = Lick For You • BM = Byte Me • HITR = Human In
The Room • WMT = Wag My Tail • RRIC = Run Round In Circles
• BSBAY = Butt Sniff Back At You • LDE = Look Doggy Eyed

love dog @dogmail.com

LOVE DOG SAYS (10:17:10AM)
WOOF WOOF BS PUP. BARK BARK DROOL HOWL BARK BARK BARK WMT HOWL BARK

FOXY TERRIER SAYS (10:17:10:02AM)
YOL :-) BSBAY BARK BARK BARK WOOF HOOOOOWWWLLL BARK BARK BARK

LOVE DOG SAYS (10:17:10:05AM)
ABS WOOOOOOOOOOOOOOFFFFFFFFFFFFFFFFFFFF! BARK ARF WOOF WOOF WOOF

SLINKY SHIH TZU SAYS (10:17:10:08AM)
LFY :-) BARK BARK BARK YIP YIP YIP WOOF BARK BARK BARK BARK YIP YIP WOOF BARK

LOVE DOG SAYS (10:17:10:10AM)
BM BARK BARK WOOF WOOF WOOF ARF ARF ARF HOOOWWWLL RRIC

POSH POODLE SAYS (10:17:10:13AM)
HITR, BARK, BARK BARK WOOF WOOF ARF ARF ARF BARK YELP YELP

LOVE DOG SAYS (10:17:10:17AM)
LDE WOOF WOOF BARK GRRRRRRRRRRRRRRRRRRR!

A 😊

Send

DAY 318

CAPTAIN JACK RUSSELL

Be **Pirates** for the day. Dress self and dog up, purchase a **parrot** and stick to dog's collar, feed him from the **treasure** chest, and speak in the present tense all day.

DAY 319

HOW SMART IS YOUR DOG?

QUESTIONS TO ASK YOUR DOG AND GET THE RIGHT ANSWER

What is the sea condition in a Force 9 gale?

ROUGH

What did a Renaissance man wear around his neck?

ROUGH

What does a tree bark feel like?

RUFF

Pawflexology

On day 185, your dog performed reflexology on you. Return the favor by massaging the bottom of his paws. Follow the maps below to see which parts of his body you are helping (we are guessing).

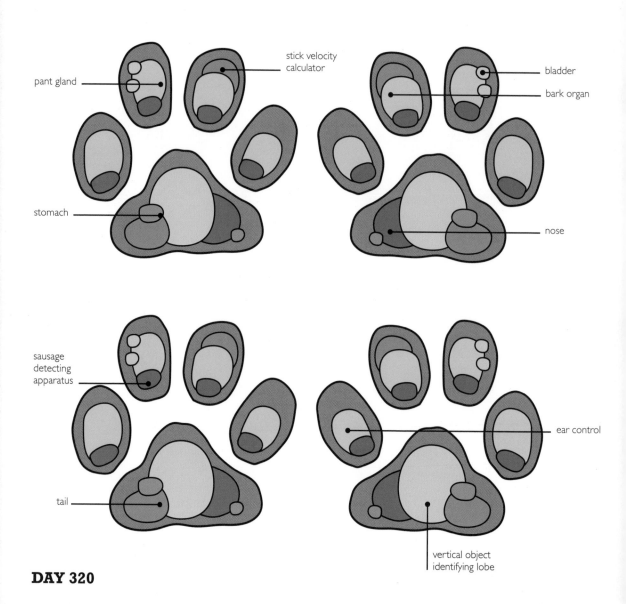

pant gland

stick velocity calculator

stomach

bladder

bark organ

nose

sausage detecting apparatus

tail

ear control

vertical object identifying lobe

DAY 320

Dog Stars No.5

This is the constellation for very smart dogs; the kind that have their own telescopes because they are smart as foxes. Some astronomers call it the Coat Hanger, but they are probably not dog owners.

Anser

Vulpecula is a northern constellation. Its name means the Little Fox and it is home to the Dumb Bell Nebula and the first ever discovered pulsar. The alpha is Anser.

VULPECULA

ME NO LAIKA

Laika the Moscow stray was rocketed into orbit in November 1957, the first dog in space. Let your dog pay homage. Wrap a KFC bucket in tin foil, cut holes for the eyes, place it on your dog's head, and point out to him how lucky he is that he was not the one orbiting the Earth and burning up in its atmosphere.

DAY 322

DAY 323
MIND GAMES

While your dog is asleep, surround his basket with doll's house furniture or model buildings. **When your dog wakes up he will think he is a giant.**

MOMMIE DEAREST

GET YOUR DOG TO CALL HIS MOTHER. WHAT IS SHE, CHOPPED LIVER?

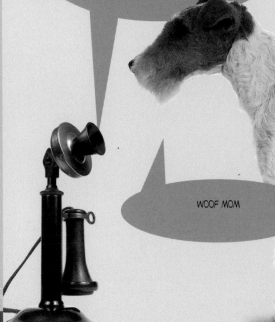

WOOF!
BARK BARK WOOF WOOF
ARF WOOF BARK BARK GRRRRR
WOOF WOOF ARF ARF WOOF WOOF
BARK BARK GRRRR YELP WOOF
WOOF ARF

WOOF MOM

DAY 324

DAY 325

HOME SHOPPING

Go online shopping with your dog. Let him bash the keyboard and buy whatever he randomly hits.

DAY 326

INSIDE OUT

ALL DOGS stick their heads out of cars to LET THEIR EARS BLOW IN THE WIND. Do your dog a favor and SIMULATE THIS EXPERIENCE in his own home, USING A CARDBOARD BOX AND A HAIRDRYER on a cold setting. Cut a hole in the side of the box so he can stick his head out, then direct the hair dryer at him.

RETRO WALKING

Similar to going forward but going backward instead; good for both you and your dog.

DOG TOPIARY

DAY 328

IMMORTALIZE YOUR PET

CUT HIS LIKENESS INTO YOUR HEDGE.

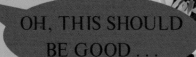

OH, THIS SHOULD BE GOOD . . .

OFFER A FIELD OF DREAMS

You don't know what your dog's inner career desires are. Maybe he feels constrained by his breed. Help him out by offering him a field of dreams. Here are two examples to inspire you:

❶ If you have a fat old bulldog, make him some greyhound racing silks and let him plod around the yard following a toy rabbit pulled on a string, very slowly.

❷ If you have a dachshund, buy him some stack-heeled boots, tie a miniature of brandy round his neck, and lie down under a large heap of polystyrene packing granules. Let him rescue you from under the avalanche.

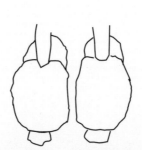

DAY 329

DAY 330

DOODLE
YOUR UPRIGHT
POODLE: 4

Here is another opportunity to hone your drawing skills. Try the front view first, then move on to the back. Note: Drawing the nether regions is advanced work, and may need some practice.

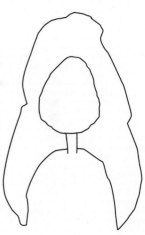

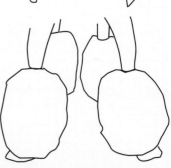

OUTSOURCE YOUR DOG'S JOBS: 7

RIDE SHOTGUN

Speedfreak wanted to ride in back of owner's car with head sticking out of rear or side window and tongue sticking out of mouth.

SKILLS REQUIRED

- Long and/or floppy ears for streaming in the wind
- Tolerance to high wind speed

ROTTWEILERS REQUIRED

As background artistes for British gangster movie shooting next month. Must be top-of-the-reed but have no discernible personality or charm so that they don't upstage the cast and the plot. **Call 555-1235-5990**

TERRIER SOUGHT

For part-time post as office dog. Must be of

DAY 332

REPURPOSE YOUR DOG 6

This is especially suitable for the older dog. Train your dog to lay along the back seat ledge of your car and to nod its head gently while you corner.

DEPUTY DAWG

Enhance your dog's citizenship skills by making him sheriff for the day. Make him a badge. Address him as Mr. Earp all day long. Probably a good idea to keep the weaponry locked up though, because he might have an itchy trigger paw.

INSULATE YOUR DOG

Measure your dog and create an insulating suit for him. It should have two layers, and contain flexible pipework in-between. Hot or cold water can be pumped in to stabilize your dog's temperature in all weather conditions. Great for winter walks or when there is a power cut and the heating/air conditioning pack up.

DAY
334

DOG LATIN

Dog Latin is mock Latin, which sounds good and scholarly but isn't, e.g. Non illegitimi carborundum (don't let the bastards grind you down). Most things sound better in Latin, so why not try it out on your dog? It is his language, after all.

WOOF! WOOF!...LATRO! LATRO!
GRRR !...FREMO!
DOWN BOY...SEDE TE
GOOD DOG...CATULE BONE
FETCH...DEPROME!
PUT IT DOWN...DEPONE ID

DOG HORTICULTURE

PLANT A HABITAT FOR YOUR DOG:
Put in only plants that have dog names or are canine related.
All these plants have been chosen because they require no care and attention, so your dog can look after them himself.

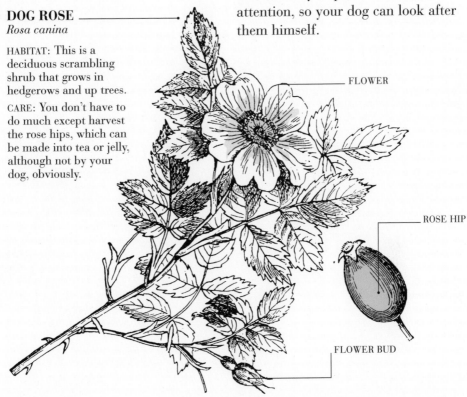

1 DOG ROSE
Rosa canina

HABITAT: This is a deciduous scrambling shrub that grows in hedgerows and up trees.

CARE: You don't have to do much except harvest the rose hips, which can be made into tea or jelly, although not by your dog, obviously.

FLOWER

ROSE HIP

FLOWER BUD

2 DOG VIOLET
Viola riviniana

HABITAT: This perennial likes short grass, woods, and wasteland, in dry habitats.

CARE: Easy-peasy; plant in the sun or semishade, wait for April, and watch the butterflies flock here.

3 DOG'S TAIL GRASS
Cynosurus cristatus

HABITAT: This perennial likes dry pastures and moist, clay soil.

CARE: Negligible; sheep love it and scarf it down. So if you want to get rid of it, hire an ovine.

4 HOUND'S TONGUE
Cynosurus cristatus

HABITAT: A mildly poisonous biennial weed, so will grow wherever it seeds.

CARE: Don't encourage it; it can damage the liver of a grazing animal, despite looking like a dog's tongue.

5 DOG DAISY
Bellis perennis

HABITAT: Called a weed by the insensitive, it thrives on short grass and lawns.

CARE: None. If you want to get rid of it, plant taller grasses, which will dwarf it.

6 DOG WOOD
Cornus sanguinea

HABITAT: This deciduous tree grows almost anywhere, but likes reasonably moist soil.

CARE: You get leaves, flowers, and berries. All it wants in return is to be loved.

7 DOG CAMOMILE
Anthemis cotula

HABITAT: An annual weed that grows on roadsides, wasteland, and in sandy soil.

CARE: Why would you want to? It stinks and tastes foul—at least to humans.

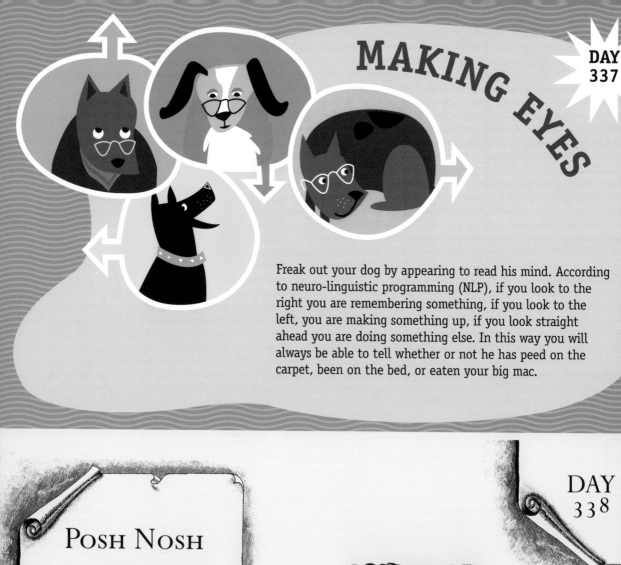

MAKING EYES

Freak out your dog by appearing to read his mind. According to neuro-linguistic programming (NLP), if you look to the right you are remembering something, if you look to the left, you are making something up, if you look straight ahead you are doing something else. In this way you will always be able to tell whether or not he has peed on the carpet, been on the bed, or eaten your big mac.

POSH NOSH

Give your dog a gourmet experience at his next meal. Serve an amuse-gueule. Arrange the main dish in a tower, with a swoosh of jus, a single chew, and a fine dusting of bonemeal. Set the food bowl on a larger underplate, preferably hexagonal. Write a menu, in French. Make your dog a place name. Wear a dinner suit yourself, and tie a napkin on him before he starts.

Mighty WURLITZER

DAY 339

Make an organ for your dog by fixing his squeaky toys along a stout stick to form a keyboard. Test them first to make sure they squeak on different notes. See how long it is before he manages a Brandenberg Variation (by Bach, naturally).

DAY 340
HAIR TODAY
Treat your dog to a Brazilian or a back crack and sack. If the HSUS (Humane Society of the United States) catches you, tell them the dog insisted.

DAY 341
BODY ART

When your dog's teeth come out, clean them up and fashion them into a necklace or bracelet for you or your dog.

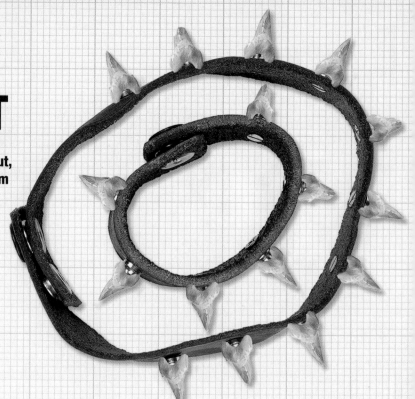

OVERSIZE
Dog Carrier

day
342

Celebs carry their teacup pooches around in handbags; but suppose you own an Irish Wolfhound or St. Bernard? Today you can solve that problem. Make a carrying bag for him out of a truck tarpaulin and that rope they tie boats to the harbor with.

Doggy JENGA

DAY 343

Build a tower of dog treats and test your dog's powers of self-control and delicacy of touch. He has to pick off one dog treat at a time without knocking them all over. If they fall down, he's not allowed to eat them. Honestly, he'll love it…

DAY 344

Take your dog to work. Let him share your day.

DAY 345

Masterclass Graduation

When you have PASSED ALL YOUR MASTERCLASSES to your dog's satisfaction, get him to stamp each section with his paw so that you have a record of your achievement.

That's my kind of dog

DAY 346

DOGSICLE

Carve your dog out of ice. You can flavor it with beef extract. Stand it in his bowl and he can lick it and drink it as it melts.

DAY 347

Dog Angel

A seasonal treat for your dog. Give the command "play dead," and both lay on your backs in the snow, arms and legs outstretched. Move legs apart and together and arms up and down to create gown, wings, etc. Persevere, even if first attempts are messy.

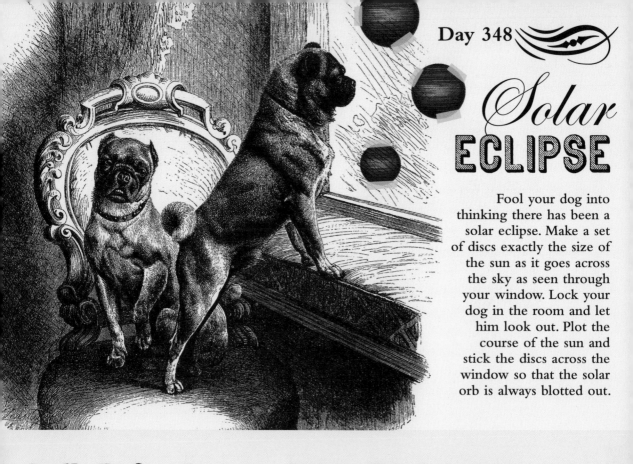

Solar ECLIPSE

Fool your dog into thinking there has been a solar eclipse. Make a set of discs exactly the size of the sun as it goes across the sky as seen through your window. Lock your dog in the room and let him look out. Plot the course of the sun and stick the discs across the window so that the solar orb is always blotted out.

DAY 349: Being John Barkovich

Is your dog consumed with Nervalesque ennui and self-loathing? Then make him a mask so he looks like a different breed, and let him enjoy someone else's personality for a change.

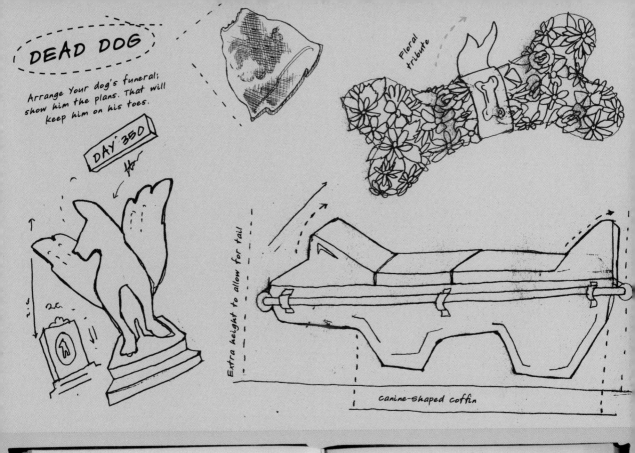

DEAD DOG

Arrange your dog's funeral; show him the plans. That will keep him on his toes.

DAY 350

Floral tribute

Extra height to allow for tail

Canine-shaped coffin

fairy story day

Today you will test the transformative power of love. Dress your dog as a frog. You can easily knit him a Frog Suit, as shown. If you can't knit, show this to someone who can and get him or her to copy it.

Then you can spend the day kissing your dog to see if he will turn into a handsome prince.

day 351

Random Fetching

Today you will jolt your dog out of tired old fetching habits. Ask friends, relatives, and fellow owners to create a list, writing down as many random objects as they can think of. Show your dog the list. Give the command "FETCH!" while pointing at the first thing on the list. Tick off each item as your dog brings it back. This could take several hours so set an agreed time limit for each item. You may help by showing him pictures of unfamiliar objects.

BONE APPETIT

DAY 353

la menu

Invite five of your dog's friends around and provide six servings of six different bones. Write down the varieties on the bones on the left. Try each one and write details of its taste, crunch, and lasting finish on the tongue. Award paw ratings (see below). Your dog should eat the five-paw bone and bury the others.

PAW RATINGS

Award a paw rating to each bone. Range from 0 paws (for a disappointing bone experience) to five paws for a superb example. The bone with most paws gets the rosette.

winner
Prix d'Or
de Chien

Your dog dreams of being a star dog. buy posters of famous dogs in film scenes, cut a hole where their heads are, get your dog to stick his head through, and then take a photograph. Suggest :Toto (Wizard of Oz), Hooch (Turner and Hooch), Frank (Men in Black)...

WANNABE

DAY
354

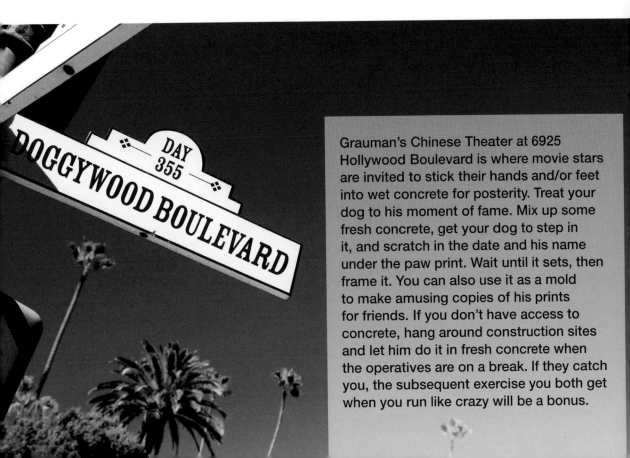

DAY
355

DOGGYWOOD BOULEVARD

Grauman's Chinese Theater at 6925 Hollywood Boulevard is where movie stars are invited to stick their hands and/or feet into wet concrete for posterity. Treat your dog to his moment of fame. Mix up some fresh concrete, get your dog to step in it, and scratch in the date and his name under the paw print. Wait until it sets, then frame it. You can also use it as a mold to make amusing copies of his prints for friends. If you don't have access to concrete, hang around construction sites and let him do it in fresh concrete when the operatives are on a break. If they catch you, the subsequent exercise you both get when you run like crazy will be a bonus.

Doggy Nasdaq

The stock market is only gambling. Your dog stands as good a chance of picking juicy stocks as any. Scratch the initials of a random set of listed companies on four sticks. Throw them. Bet on the one the dog brings back. If he's right, give him a bonus and a top-of-the-range Frisbee.

DAY 356

Imaginary best friend

You have imaginary friends. Perhaps your dog does as well, but is unable to tell you about them. Help him out by:

- Providing extra bowls of food and water
- Buying an extra leash
- Throwing sticks, balls etc., for the imaginary dog
- Patting the air next to your dog
- Driving with both back windows open.

DAY 357

DAY 358

COLOR CODING

DYE YOUR DOG a different color for each day of the week

YOUR DOG

TUESDAY

THURSDAY

SATURDAY

DAY 359

GET TOGETHER

IT'S THANKSGIVING.
Invite your dog's mother,
father if possible, siblings
and puppies (if any) for a get
together with turkey and
everything. If you don't
do Thanksgiving, substitute
the fraught family festival
of your choice.

Ghostdog

TELL EVERYONE YOUR DOG IS DEAD. Have a wake. It'll be fun and lend verisimilitude, although you will have to put your dog in kennels, preferably in another town while you go through the motions.

Collect your dog and smuggle him back home. Comb him through with talcum powder for a suitable spectral effect. Take him out for a walk along a route where you know you will meet friends. Look sad and let the leash hang slack in your hand. When you meet your friends, say mournfully that you cannot help retracing old walks with his old leash, even though he is no longer with you.

DAY 360

Dog nose prints

🐾 Did you know that dogs' nose prints are as unique as human fingerprints? In Canada there has been a database of dog nose prints in use since 1938. To prevent your dog being falsely arrested for a crime, why not take his nose prints yourself and store them in a safe place?

1) Black dog's nose using genuine fingerprint ink
2) Roll nose over pad of paper
3) Label and date

TIP: For extra security, get your dog to sign the nose print with his pawmark.

DAY 361

TALK TO YOUR DOG
IN HIS OWN LANGUAGE

6: Play Dead

Lay down on your back with legs and arms in the air and eyes closed. Hang your tongue out if you like. Stay as still as you can, even when your dog sniffs your butt.

INSTANT DOG YEARS CALCULATOR

It is a common belief that one human year is equal to seven dog years. That is not very accurate, since dogs reach adulthood within the first couple of years. The formula is: 10.5 dog years per human year for the first two years, then four dog years per human year for each year after. You do the math. Or maybe you should let your dog do it.

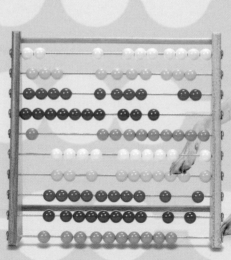

DAY
363

DAY 364

7 TODAY!

It is seven years, in dog years, since you and your dog started on this project. Plus you are one year older.

Celebrate together
Make a cake
Give a gift
Send a card
Prepare a special treat
Organize an outing
Invite friends round
Crack open the champagne

HAPPY 7TH BIRTHDAY

Evaluation DAY

DAY 365

Congratulations! You have completed your joint journey of self-transformation. Now it's time to reflect. Go back over the year with your dog and discuss what was the most life-changing thing you did together. Then let us know and we will incorporate the information into our *This Book Will Change Your Dog's Life* database for future reference. In this way you will make a contribution toward changing the lives of dogs everywhere!

FOR THEIR *STIMULATING* SUGGESTIONS,
GRATEFUL THANKS TO:

WAYNE BLADES, SOPHIE COLLINS, CAROLINE EARLE, EMMA FRITH,
RICHARD GOGARTY, LORRAINE HARRISON, JASON HOOK,
STEVE KNOWLDEN, ANNA STEVENS, HELEN TOOKEY, LORRAINE TURNER,
MICHAEL WHITEHEAD.

SPECIAL THANKS TO TED THE OFFICE DOG,
WITHOUT WHOSE UNFLAGGING ENTHUSIASM AND SELFLESS
WILLINGNESS TO BENCH-TEST ALL OUR SUGGESTIONS, THIS BOOK
WOULD NEVER HAVE GOT STARTED.

Ted: unflagging enthusiasm

NOTE

Throughout this book we have referred to your dog as "he." Now, we know that 50 percent of dogs at least are shes, but there is not a lot of room to keep on with the he-or-she business and no dog lover would ever call their dog "it." On the grounds that we believe few lady dogs would be fooled into doing the things outlined in this book, we have gone with "he" throughout.

PICTURE CREDITS
Bridgeman Art Library/National Gallery, London, UK: page 23; Private collection: page 122T.
Corbis/Bettmann: page 9CL, page 9CR, page 117B, page 118B; Hubert Boesl/dpa: page 9R; Owen Franken: page 32B.